Savannah Cats as Pets

A Complete Savannah Cat Owner Guide

Savannah Cat Breeding, Where to Buy, Types, Care, Temperament, Cost, Health, Showing, Grooming, Diet and Much More Included!

By Lolly Brown

Foreword

The Savannah hybrid cat is quickly becoming one of the most popular cat breeds in the world. If you have seen one of these beauties and wondered whether it would suit you as a pet, this book provides you with many of the information you will need to determine whether you are suited to caring for one of these cats, and what it means to actually take care of one.

In recent years, since the Savannah cat was first introduced into the world, public opinion has ranged from appreciation to cautious wariness. Some have fallen in love with these cats, while others are wary at bringing home what may be a half-wild cat. Yes, Savannah cats are not like domestic cats - they are, after all, hybrid cats. But they can coexist quite well with a human family, provided the human family knows the peculiar quirks, traits and needs of a Savannah cat. More than with most domestic cat breeds, you have to know what you're getting into before you take the plunge with one of these guys. Many times, an owner forced to surrender one of these cats to shelters simply did not know what he or she was getting into when she brought one of these cats home.

Armed with the proper knowledge, and the willingness and commitment for caring for a Savannah, having one in your home can be a very fulfilling adventure.

Table of Contents

Introduction

In recent years, many hybrid wild cats have caught the public's attention. They are noted for their beautiful wild look and their domesticated temperament. The Savannah cat - the original of which descended from a natural mating between the African Serval and a domestic Siamese cat - is one of these gorgeous hybrid cats that are fast growing in popularity among cat owners and cat enthusiasts worldwide.

Savannah cats are high energy cats that love water and are great climbers - some can jump as high as the highest point in your house. They are also pretty fast runners. But along with these natural skills inherited from their wild ancestry, Savannahs are one of the most loving, goofy and comic cat breeds around. They are energetic, loving, funny, and with a great sense of humor. They are also highly intelligent, and may continually surprise you not only with how many tricks you can teach it, but also with how many things it begins to figure out on its own - such as opening drawers, turning on faucets, and jumping out at you to surprise you.

But owning a Savannah cat also entails a huge responsibility, and a lifelong commitment. Simply put, Savannah cats are not for everyone. While they are highly sought after and are very much in demand, the first thing you should ask yourself is whether or not you are capable of caring for a Savannah in the way that it deserves to be taken care of? This, and more, information is presented to you in this book - from tips on nutrition and diet, grooming, training, and even the possible health conditions of the breed, this book is a comprehensive guide for both new and old Savannah cat owners.

Glossary of Cat Terms

Abundism – Referring to a cat that has markings more prolific than is normal.

Acariasis – A type of mite infection.

ACF – Australian Cat Federation

Affix – A cattery name that follows the cat's registered name; cattery owner, not the breeder of the cat.

Agouti – A type of natural coloring pattern in which individual hairs have bands of light and dark coloring.

Ailurophile – A person who loves cats.

Albino – A type of genetic mutation which results in little to no pigmentation, in the eyes, skin, and coat.

Allbreed – Referring to a show that accepts all breeds or a judge who is qualified to judge all breeds.

Alley Cat – A non-pedigreed cat.

Alter – A desexed cat; a male cat that has been neutered or a female that has been spayed.

Amino Acid – The building blocks of protein; there are 22 types for cats, 11 of which can be synthesized and 11 which must come from the diet (see essential amino acid).

Anestrus – The period between estrus cycles in a female cat.

Any Other Variety (AOV) – A registered cat that doesn't conform to the breed standard.

ASH – American Shorthair, a breed of cat.

Back Cross – A type of breeding in which the offspring is mated back to the parent.

Balance – Referring to the cat's structure; proportional in accordance with the breed standard.

Barring – Describing the tabby's striped markings.

Base Color – The color of the coat.

Bicolor – A cat with patched color and white.

Blaze – A white coloring on the face, usually in the shape of an inverted V.

Bloodline – The pedigree of the cat.

Brindle – A type of coloring, a brownish or tawny coat with streaks of another color.

Castration – The surgical removal of a male cat's testicles.

Cat Show – An event where cats are shown and judged.

Cattery – A registered cat breeder; also, a place where cats may be boarded.

CFA – The Cat Fanciers Association.

Cobby – A compact body type.

Colony – A group of cats living wild outside.

Color Point – A type of coat pattern that is controlled by color point alleles; pigmentation on the tail, legs, face, and ears with an ivory or white coat.

Colostrum – The first milk produced by a lactating female; contains vital nutrients and antibodies.

Conformation – The degree to which a pedigreed cat adheres to the breed standard.

Cross Breed – The offspring produced by mating two distinct breeds.

Dam – The female parent.

Declawing – The surgical removal of the cat's claw and first toe joint.

Developed Breed – A breed that was developed through selective breeding and crossing with established breeds.

Down Hairs – The short, fine hairs closest to the body which keep the cat warm.

DSH – Domestic Shorthair.

Estrus – The reproductive cycle in female cats during which she becomes fertile and receptive to mating.

Fading Kitten Syndrome – Kittens that die within the first two weeks after birth; the cause is generally unknown.

Feral – A wild, untamed cat of domestic descent.

Gestation – Pregnancy; the period during which the fetuses develop in the female's uterus.

Guard Hairs – Coarse, outer hairs on the coat.

Harlequin – A type of coloring in which there are van markings of any color with the addition of small patches of the same color on the legs and body.

Inbreeding – The breeding of related cats within a closed group or breed.

Kibble – Another name for dry cat food.

Lilac – A type of coat color that is pale pinkish-gray.

Line – The pedigree of ancestors; family tree.

Litter – The name given to a group of kittens born at the same time from a single female.

Mask – A type of coloring seen on the face in some breeds.

Matts – Knots or tangles in the cat's fur.

Mittens – White markings on the feet of a cat.

Moggie – Another name for a mixed breed cat.

Mutation – A change in the DNA of a cell.

Mutation Breed – A breed of cat that resulted from a spontaneous mutation; ex: Cornish Rex and Sphynx.

Muzzle – The nose and jaws of an animal.

Natural Breed – A breed that developed without selective breeding or the assistance of humans.

Neutering – Desexing a male cat.

Open Show – A show in which spectators are allowed to view the judging.

Pads – The thick skin on the bottom of the feet.

Particolor – A type of coloration in which there are markings of two or more distinct colors.

Patched – A type of coloration in which there is any solid color, tabby, or tortoiseshell color plus white.

Pedigree – A purebred cat; the cat's papers showing its family history.

Pet Quality – A cat that is not deemed of high enough standard to be shown or bred.

Piebald – A cat with white patches of fur.

Points – Also color points; markings of contrasting color on the face, ears, legs, and tail.

Pricked – Referring to ears that sit upright.

Purebred – A pedigreed cat.

Queen – An intact female cat.

Roman Nose – A type of nose shape with a bump or arch.

Scruff – The loose skin on the back of a cat's neck.

Selective Breeding – A method of modifying or improving a breed by choosing cats with desirable traits.

Senior – A cat that is more than 5 but less than 7 years old.

Sire – The male parent of a cat.

Solid – Also self; a cat with a single coat color.

Spay – Desexing a female cat.

Stud – An intact male cat.

Tabby – A type of coat pattern consisting of a contrasting color over a ground color.

Tom Cat – An intact male cat.

Tortoiseshell – A type of coat pattern consisting of a mosaic of red or cream and another base color.

Tri-Color – A type of coat pattern consisting of three distinct colors in the coat.

Tuxedo – A black and white cat.

Unaltered – A cat that has not been desexed.

Chapter One: Understanding Savannah Cats

Most people dreaming of owning a Savannah cat may be wondering whether it is a good cat breed for them. This is a legitimate question, as not everybody is suitable or has the capacity to take care of one of these gorgeous hybrid cats. So before you go out and shell out big money for one of these cats, the first thing you should do is gather information, research, and honestly and objectively assess yourself as a prospective Savannah cat breeder. Most of the things that will decide you will be the peculiar needs, characteristics, and traits of the Savannah cat, and your capacity to provide these for them.

This chapter provides you a brief overview of the popular Savannah cat, a summary of the facts regarding this hybrid breed, and its history. Read on, and enjoy the process of getting to know one of the most recent hybrid cats in the world.

Facts About Savannah Cats

The very first Savannah cat came from a natural and unintended mating between a wild African Serval and a domesticated Siamese cat. The result of this mating was a beautiful female kitten named "Savannah" - after the African grasslands that are the home of its parent, the African Serval.

Since then, the development of the breed has been brought about by the dedication, commitment and persistence of many breeders working hand in hand, not only to produce the best kind of Savannah cat hybrid, but also in the promotion of this breed - which has now been accepted by The International Cat Association (TICA) as a Championship Breed.

But the Savannah cat is not for everyone. This is a high energy, very active cat that is a powerful jumper and with a sense of humor to spare. Anyone thinking of bringing home a Savannah has to be able to provide this cat the space and room it needs to thrive - including a secure enclosure outdoors, as well as vertical space for climbing. Added to that, Savannah cats require attention - as they will be constantly active and ready to play. This is not a cat you can leave alone at home for long periods of time. A responsible Savannah cat owner must have the time and dedication to provide this cat with the exercise and mental stimulation it needs - with occasional leashed walks, as well as lots of interactive playtime. This is important because if the Savannah cat has no outlet upon which to expend its considerable energy, all that energy can quickly become destructive.

With the proper attention and care, however, the Savannah cat is one of the most loving, loyal and affectionate breeds out there - to rival some of the best cat breeds, and even some of the best dog breeds out there. Yes, Savannah cats are not unlike dogs in the kind of loving bond they develop with their family. Give this cat a proper home and all the care and attention it needs, and it can be a fun and loving companion in your house for many years to come.

Summary of Savannah Cat Facts

Pedigree: original cross between an African Serval and a Siamese domestic cat, also Bengals, Egyptian Maus, Oriental Shorthairs, Ocicats, and some average domestic shorthairs

Breed Size: varies depending on generation and sex; F1 hybrid males, and F1 and F2 generations, are considered the largest,

Weight: first generation Savannahs average at 8-20 lbs (6.3-11.3 kg); later generation Savannahs' average weight average at 7-15 lbs (3.17-6.8 kg.)

Body Type: long and leggy, tall and lanky

Coat Length: medium-length, spotted coat

Coat Texture: dense coat that can be either coarse or soft in texture

Coat Color: accepted colors are brown spotted tabby, silver spotted tabby, black, and smoke; other color patterns, though considered undesirable, include rosettes, marbles, white lockets, white toes

Eyes: medium sized eyes, set underneath slightly hooded brows; top of the eye resembles a boomerang, set at an angle so the corner of the eye slopes down the line of the nose, the bottom half has an almond shape

Ears: largest and high on the head, wide, with a deep base; upright and with rounded tips; they are considered the largest ears of all felines, in relationship to head size

Tail: short tail with black rings, and a solid black tip

Temperament: intelligent, energetic, exuberant, outgoing, demanding of human interaction

Strangers: friendly with strangers, either curious or playful

Children: tolerant and friendly with children, though exercise due caution and supervision, especially with infants and very small children

Other Pets: playful and gets along well with dogs and most other pets, but exercise due caution and supervision when it comes to smaller pets

Exercise Needs: needs daily exercise, sufficient vertical territory (cat trees), and daily interactive play with humans and/or other active pets

Health Conditions: generally healthy with no known genetic or breed-specific diseases or conditions

Lifespan: average 13-20 years

Savannah Cat Breed History

The first documented Savannah cat was born on April 7, 1986. A female Siamese cat owned by Judee Frank gave birth to a female kitten sired by an Serval - a wild African cat. She eventually came to be owned by breeder Suzi Wood, who named this unplanned for offspring "Savannah"

- after the African grasslands which Servals originally called home. Savannah later on became the name of the breed itself.

Suzi Wood wrote two articles about Savannah, and caught the interest of Patrick Kelley, who was interested in starting a new breed of domestic cat with a wild spotted look. Neither of Savannah's former owners, Judee Frank or Suzi Wood, were interested however, so Patrick Kelley contacted several breeders, among whom was Joyce Sroufe, to help in his efforts. Patrick Kelley bought the only female kitten in Savannah's litter, and thus began the F2 and F3 generations of Savannahs. Both Patrick Kelley and Joyce Sroufe wrote the original Breed Standard, which they presented to the TICA (The International Cat Association) on February 1996.

Joyce's Sroufe's efforts and dedication proved fertile - she was able to produce more Savannahs than any other breeder, and to produce the first fertile male Savannahs. She introduced this breed to the public for the first time during an exhibition at a cat show in Westchester, New York, in 1997. She is now considered to be the Founder of the Savannah Breed.

Meanwhile, Patrick Kelley worked continuously to promote the recognition and acceptance of the Savannah as a breed. When TICA lifted their moratorium on new breeds, the Savannah was accepted for registration and granted Experimental New Breed Status.

Lorre Smith, the first TICA Savannah Breed Chairperson, also helped in the promotion and recognition of this breed. She worked tirelessly even during TICA's moratorium on hybrid breeds, which resulted the quick forward launch of Savannahs within the ranks of TICA breeds. After the moratorium was lifted, Savannahs were accepted into TICA's New Breed program.

Savannahs rose quickly through the ranks, moving from "Experimental New Breed," to "Preliminary New Breed," and finally to "Advanced New Breed." In 2012, TICA granted the Savannahs Championship status.

During the development of the breed, a spotted coat was considered desirable (and is the only pattern accepted by the TICA standard), and so there were outcrosses to other spotted cat breedsincluding Bengals, Egyptian Maus, Oriental Shorthairs, Ocicat, and some average domestic shorthairs. Now that the breed is established, however, outcrossing is no longer permitted.

In the years since then, the response of the public, including TICA Judges, were overwhelmingly favorable to Savannah cats. Despite their rarity, they are one of the most popular and sought after cat breeds today.

Chapter Two: Things to Know Before Getting a Savannah Cat

It is very easy to be dazzled by the beauty of its recently-developed cat that it is sometimes easy to forget about some of the more mundane aspects of Savannah cat ownership. But if you wish to be a responsible Savannah cat owner, no detail should be too small. In this chapter, we take a look at some of the more practical aspects of owning a Savannah cat, including the legality of ownership, the

possible need for licenses or permits, and the specific
requirements for transporting a Savannah cat between states
or countries. We also take a look at the costs of keeping a
Savannah, and an overview of the pros and cons of the
breed.

Do You Need a License or a Special Permit?

Like with most domestic cats, the regulations and
laws governing ownership of Savannah cats varies from
state to state, and even from country to country. It is
imperative that you check with your local legislative
agencies to determine the legality of Savannah cat
ownership, since it is illegal to own them in some states and
countries. And because state laws can change over time,
sometimes even faster than we think, it might be a good idea
to stay constantly updated to check whether any changes in
the laws might add restrictions or affect the legality of your
pet ownership.

The first thing you have to check is how Savannah
cats are classified. In general, Savannahs are considered
hybrid wild cats, not domestic cats, although in some states,
later generations of Savannahs are already considered
domestic cats (usually F6 and onwards). In certain states

that restrict ownership of Savannahs, no more than F3, F4 or later generations of Savannah cats are allowed, while F1 to F2 or F3 that are considered wild animal hybrids are illegal to own, or may require stricter regulations such as on ownership and accommodation (e.g., must be caged).

Be sure to check not just your state law but also your local county law. Local bylaws of town/city may still ban hybrids even if county and state law allows them. For instance, New York state allows ownership of F6 and later generations of Savannahs, but they are not allowed in NYC. Needless to say, this can be a potentially chaotic situation if you find out that your local area prohibits or restricts ownership of Savannah cats even if your state law does not. A similar situation exists in Canada, where provinces such as Alberta and Saskatchewan have specific restrictions on hybrid cats

As of this writing, states which prohibit or restrict ownership of hybrid cat ownership include Hawaii, Massachusetts, and Georgia. Hybrid cats are also prohibited in Australia, due to local concerns for the native wildlife, which are already being threatened by domestic feral cats. In the UK, Serval and F1 Savannah cat ownership requires a special license, while later generations of Savannah cats are essentially legal and require no special license or permit. So before you even buy a Savannah cat, do your due diligence, as even transporting or importing Savannah cats may also fall under specific regulations.

CITES, or the Convention on International Trade in Endangered Species of Wild Fauna and Flora, apply here since Savannah cats are considered covered by CITES. Transporting Savannah cats between or across international borders therefore require a permit. Traveling with your Savannah across borders also requires a CITES pet passport. Failure to abide among the 170 member nations of CITES means confiscation of your cat, which will most likely not be returned. Take note that international transport also requires a USDA health certificate and a fish and wildlife inspection of your cat. Rabies vaccines should also be up to date.

Do Savannah Cats Get Along with Other Pets?

Provided there was proper socialization experience during the first few weeks of the kitten's life, and provided a continuing atmosphere of positive socialization at home, Savannah cats can make great buddies with other pets, such as dogs and other cats. Their playful and affectionate nature make them great buddies with other pets at home.

A proviso should be made, however, when it comes to other smaller animals such as rats, mice, birds, fish, and other similar animals that may naturally be considered the natural prey of cats. If you do keep these types of pets, proper supervision should always be exercised.

How Many Savannah Cats Should You Keep?

The decision of whether or not you can keep more than one Savannah cat is up to you and your capacity for caring for more than one cat. Remember that this is an expensive breed, and the costs of caring for them and boarding then, not to mention the energy investment in their regular grooming, nutrition and diet, and games and exercise, might also take its toll on some.

On the other hand, because the Savannah cat is demanding of attention and energy, some owners do recommend keeping more than one Savannah cat. This gives your cat a buddy with whom to play with and socialize, thus continually honing his abilities of interacting with other cats, while giving him another playmate - something that can spare owners who are starved of the time it takes to give the Savannah cat the attention that they need.

If you are bringing home a female and a male, and you are not intending to breed, please remember to have your cats neutered or spayed. Also exercise due supervision even if you are bringing home cats of the same gender, or of different age ranges, or even of different breeds. It does not happen often, but sometimes friction can happen even among housemates. Weigh the options, and decide accordingly.

How Much Does it Cost to Keep a Savannah Cat?

Savannahs are one of the most expensive cat breeds around - and this is mostly because of the comparative rarity of the breed, and the difficulty of the process of breeding them. It isn't easy to breed Savannah cats, and most male Savannahs are sterile until the fourth generation, sometimes even later. Fertile males fetch a hefty price, and so do fertile females of an earlier generation.

But the cost of keeping a Savannah cat is not limited to the initial purchase price. You also have to think about their food, veterinary health checks and vaccines, and the various miscellaneous costs including toys, accessories, and even the wear and tear and damage to house furniture - and the costs can easily skyrocket. In this chapter, we present you with a general guideline of the costs of keeping a Savannah cat. Keep in mind that these are all estimates, and can easily be higher or lower depending on your area, and the cost of products and services in your region.

Initial Costs

Expect to shell out more during your first year of Savannah cat ownership. Aside from the purchase price, costs of transport, registration, and the costs of licensing or permits, you will also have to invest in the cat's vaccinations, spaying or neutering, veterinary checks, microchipping, and the purchase of the various tools and equipment you will need such as pet beds, food and water bowls, an assortment of cat toys and furniture such as scratching posts and others. Also factor in the costs of any changes you will be making in your home for these cats, such as a secure cat enclosure in your yard.

If you are thinking of adopting a Savannah cat, you might be able to find one after paying the adoption fee which can range from $100 to 300. The cost of a purebred kitten bought direct from the buyer, however, can vary between generations and among breeders. Simply put, because the Savannah cat is so much in demand among cat owners these days, the price can be pretty steep, ranging anywhere from $2,000 to $18,000 and yes, sometimes even higher.

Annual Costs

Don't forget that you will also need to pay for the regular annual expenses such as food, litter and litter boxes, veterinarian fees, grooming fees, and other similar expenses. If you are keeping more than one Savannah cat, doubling those expenses is a good estimate, though you might want to add in a little leeway just in case.

Below is a simple table to show you some of the initial and annual costs you will have to budget for if you plan to bring home a Savannah cat.

Item	Initial Costs	Annual Costs
Initial Purchase Price	$2,000-18,000 (£1, 540-13,860)	
Pet Equipment and Accessories	$250 (£193.05)	
Microchipping	$20-25 (£15.44-19.31)	
Food		$250-310 (£193.05-239.38)
Cat Litter		$75-150 (£57.92-115.83)
Veterinarian Fees, Spaying or	$130-170 (£100.39-131.27)	

Neutering		
Vaccinations	$50 (£38.61)	
Worming		$50-75 (£38.61-57.92)
Flea Treatment		$75 (£57.92)
Veterinarian Fees		$50-65 (£38.61-50.19)
Insurance		$95-235 (£73.36-181.47)
Grooming and other miscellaneous expenses		$250-645 (£193.05-498.07)

*Costs may vary depending on location
**U.K. prices based on an estimated exchange of $1 = £0.90

It is a safe bet to say that you will probably have to budget an average of about $1,000 monthly for a single Savannah cat. Again, this can actually be cheaper depending on your lifestyle and the prices in your area for services and products, but probably not by too much, as there might always be various unforeseen emergencies cropping up that you will have to factor in. It is highly recommended, in fact, that you set aside a pet emergency fund to draw from whenever those unforeseen emergencies transpire and you need to shell out additional funds for the care of your cat.

What are the Pros and Cons of Savannah Cats?

So to sum it all up, here is a brief overview of some of the pros and cons of the Savannah cat hybrid breed. Read them carefully, and honestly assess your capacity for caring for one of these cats. If you are leaning more towards the cons, this breed is probably not the right one for you. It takes a unique and dedicated pet owner to provide the right kind of home for one of these unique cats.

Pros for the Savannah Cat Breed

- The Savannah is a graceful, beautiful cat with a wild look but has been bred down from its wild ancestor, the Serval. They are highly intelligent, with a sense of humor to spare. You'll probably find yourself dealing with a cat that likes pulling pranks around the house - such as dropping things down on you from where it has jumped on the shelf, or head butting you from behind when you didn't even know he was in the room. Life can be fun and full of adventure when sharing a home with one of these cats.

- A Savannah cat can be "dog-like" in its temperament in that it bonds closely with its human family, displaying great loyalty and devotion. You'll find one following you around, unwilling to be separated from you. Many Savannahs can be taught a few simple tricks such as sit, stay, fetch, lie down, etc. Properly raised and cared for, having a Savannah in the house can be a fulfilling and satisfying experience.

Cons for the Savannah Cat Breed

- Big cats that require a lot of space - vertical and running around space. They are high energy cats, great climbers, and some are intelligent enough to open drawers and doors. You need a spacious home, with a secure cat enclosure outdoors for one of these cats. They are mainly indoor cats, but they will not thrive in small spaces or apartments.

- Savannahs are very active and energetic, and they demand constant attention. They like interactive games and play, and will occasionally pull a prank on their owners. If you don't have the time to devote to them when they are looking for attention (or if they don't have any other cat to play with), all that great energy can turn destructive. If you are out of the house most of the time, or if you spend most of your time on work and don't have time to devote to

socializing with and playing with this cat, then this is
probably not the breed for you.

- Early generation Savannahs, and even some of the
  later generations, still have their wild ancestry
  dominant in their personality. Some have been
  known to hunt, stalk and kill smaller animals in the
  surrounding areas - which will not work if you live in
  a busy neighborhood with other pet owners. There
  have been some Savannahs (not all) reported to have
  become "wild" after reaching the age of sexual
  maturity. Some experience or knowledge of the
  behavior of cats in the wild is necessary when such a
  situation happens, though many experts say that such
  behavior can be traced back to poor socialization
  training and processes. Continuous and ongoing
  socialization and training is, therefore, necessary in
  caring for a Savannah cat.

Chapter Three: Purchasing Your Savannah Cat

Compared to some of the more common domestic cat breeds, Savannah cats are still pretty rare, and not available worldwide. And because of this cat's sudden rise to popularity, the high demand for such a hybrid cat, and the high cost of purchasing one, it isn't always easy to tell whether you're dealing with a reputable breeder or one who's only in it for the money. And this is a pretty crucial distinction, because it can tell you whether you're going to be getting a healthy Savannah kitten who has been properly weaned, bred from healthy and temperamentally suitable parents, and properly socialized before being turned over to its new owner - you. It has been said that the first few weeks of a kitten's life pretty much determines what kind of cat it will be for the rest of its life. So getting a Savannah cat from a breeder who knows what he's doing, was able to give the kittens the proper nurturing and care it needed early on, and has knowledge and experience enough to assess whether you are a good fit for a Savannah cat of which particular generation, can actually save you a lot of frustration and heartache later on. Despite the high demand and great popularity of this breed, the Savannah cat is not for everyone.

In this chapter, we take a look at some of the options you can explore as you search for that Savannah kitten just for you.

Where Can You Buy Savannah Cats?

Before you start plunking down money for a purebred Savannah kitten, you might want to explore the possibility of adopting a rescue. The sad truth of it is that despite the recent development of the Savannah breed, the growing number of irresponsible breeders and owners who lack the commitment needed to care for their Savannah cats have resulted in a growing number of Savannah cats appearing in rescues and shelters. Many were simply surrendered because the owners found that they could no longer deal with the unique behavioral traits of the

Savannah - things they should have already learned before bringing one home!

If you are willing to put in the time, energy, effort and commitment to care for one of these special cats, and if you have the resources and the capacity (and the space) that would be ideal to make a home for a Savannah, then there is simply no reason why you should not explore the possibility of adopting one who was abandoned by its owner simply for being what it is. For one thing, adopting from a shelter is a lot cheaper than purchasing one directly from a breeder. For another thing, there are a growing number of Savannah cats ending up in shelters who simply need an owner who gets what it means to care for one of them. You'll be giving one of these gorgeous cats a home, and likely saving their life, too. You might surprise yourself and find one that's a perfect fit for you!

If adopting a rescue appeals to you, then by all means you should explore this avenue first. Below are some resources to get you started:

Savannah Cat Rescue. <http://svrescue.com/>

Sanura Exotics.
<http://www.hybridsavannahcats.com/adult_savannah_c ats.htm>

Texas Exotic Cat Rescue.
<http://awos.petfinder.com/shelters/TX1208.html>

Understandably, rescuing a mature Savannah that may or may not have behavioral problems is not an option for everyone - and some would rather pay the expensive price for a Savannah kitten that comes from a reputable breeder if it means a well-adjusted cat. But there's the rub. How can you tell that you are dealing with a reputable breeder in the first place?

Since TICA is, at present, the only cat organization that recognizes and accepts the Savannah as a distinct breed, it is probably a good idea to check the list of TICA-registered breeders on their website. Be aware, however, that TICA does not warrant any of the breeders listed on their site - and openly encourages prospective cat owners to exercise due discernment and caution when contacting any breeder. The simple fact of it is that even TICA does not have the resources to check each and every one of the catteries that have registered with them - even if they have signed the TICA Code of Ethics.

How to Choose a Reputable Savannah Cat Breeder

So how can you tell whether you're dealing with a reputable Savannah cat breeder? Finding one that is registered with TICA is probably a good starting point. But in narrowing down your leads, here are a few tips and advice to guide you as you look for the right breeder:

- The breeder will be competent enough to talk about the litter's history and pedigree. Each kitten should come with its own registration form, and the breeder should be willing enough to discuss with you the kitten's history, the stud and the queen that produced this litter, how many litters the queen and/or the stud has produced, what generation the kittens are, and how you should go about registering your own kitten with TICA.

- Some familiarity with the stud and the queen should also be in order - what you are looking for is a good background on the parents, their health history, breeding history, and even their unique temperaments. During this exchange, you should be able to tell whether the breeder genuinely cares about his Savannah cats, and how much care was taken in the selection of the parents, and how the breeding, pregnancy, queening, and the weaning process went. Don't be afraid to ask all the questions you have - a good breeder will be more than willing to answer them for you.

- While no breeder will be able to give you a 100% health guarantee on your kitten - a breeder telling you that your cat is 100% healthy should already be a warning sign - the basic health checks should already have been done. Be prepared to discuss vaccinations, deworming, and even spaying or neutering. A good breeder will be very interested in the welfare of your kitten, and should also encourage you to call whenever you have any questions or concerns.

- Be prepared to answer questions propounded to you, too. A responsible breeder wants their kittens to end up with a good home - and because Savannahs are pretty unique in the kinds of homes and owners they would be good with - the breeder might be asking you questions about your lifestyle, how many other pets you have, the type of house you live in and what accommodations the kitten will be living in, etc. Given the recent spate of Savannah cats being surrendered to shelters, responsible breeders have been screening more rigorously as to which owners can and should be allowed to own Savannah cats. Don't be offended by this - just as you're making sure that he's legit, he's doing the same with you, too.

- It's probably a safe bet not to consider purchasing a Savannah cat from a breeder that breeds more than 2 other cats. Savannah cats take a lot of energy, time and attention. If your breeder's cattery produces more than a few purebreed cats, it probably isn't a sign that he knows what he's doing - but rather a sign that he may be spreading himself a little too thin, and not able to give each litter of kitten the kind of care and attention that they deserve and need.

- A reputable Savannah breeder will not sugarcoat the merits of the breed and gloss over their less-than-fine points. Each cat has its merits and demerits, its good points and bad. It all comes with the package. Being able to take proper care of a Savannah cat means knowing precisely what it means to care for one - and a good breeder will expect you to have done your own research, too.

- A reputable breeder will be quite willing to show you the premises of his cattery, or to take you on a tour of their facilities. Look around. Is it clean, do the animals look well-taken care of, are they properly socialized and naturally curious and friendly about you? Do the cats have a natural outdoor enclosure in which they can exercise? Cats that are easily spooked and seem unaccepting of strangers might be a warning sign that the kittens are being raised without any proper socialization.

- And finally, a reputable breeder should be willing to take back your kitten if you should ever find yourself unable to take care of it. This is really after the fact, of course, and one that you'll probably never have to recourse to if you yourself are willing to put in the full responsibility and commitment of Savannah cat ownership.

Tips for Selecting a Healthy Savannah Kitten

Once you have found the right breeder, the only thing remaining is to wait for your kitten. It is likely that you are going to be asked to pay a deposit or reservation fee. And given the current popularity and high demand for Savannah cats, it is also likely that you will find yourself listed at the tag end of a waiting list. If so, just be patient. Getting a cat isn't a matter of simple shopping, after all.

Once the litter is born, and the weeks before they are fully weaned are approaching, you might be wondering how to best select the kitten that is right for you. You will be living with this kitten for the cat's entire lifespan, after all, so it is only reasonable that you think carefully about how to pick your kitten. Besides which, it is always a good idea to make sure that you are getting a healthy and well-adjusted kitten before you even bring them home. Below are a few guidelines you can follow as you make the acquaintance of the kittens for the first time:

- A healthy kitten should have a clean coat, bright, clear eyes, clean and pink ears, and a well-filled out body. Beware of signs of sneezing or sniffling, discharges in the corners of the eyes, or signs of flea dirt at the base of the tail - which can look like small patches of black sand.

- A well-socialized kitten should be naturally curious and playful, not too forward or aggressive, friendly, active, and not averse to being held. That means that there has been enough socialization between the kitten and its siblings to teach him his boundaries, and between the kitten and the breeder to ensure proper socialization with humans.

- Needless to say, the kitten should, by now be fully weaned. He should no longer be nursing from his mother, but is fully capable of eating on his own. And while you may not have occasion to see this for yourself - a kitten should already be competent with the uses of the litter box. You might want to ask the breeder about this, and whether the kitten has any quirks regarding this - such as sharing a litter box with his siblings, or separate boxes for his pee and poop.

- The kitten must have already had its first shots - and the breeder will provide you with the proper records for this, including a schedule of the subsequent vaccinations needed.

Savannah-Proofing Your Home

More commonly-referred to as kitten-proofing your home, Savannah-proofing is not unlike baby-proofing, or kitten-proofing, in that you have to ensure that your home is safe for your Savannah kitten. The only difference is that you have to take into account the Savannah's considerable climbing ability, as well as their characteristic curiosity, playfulness, and high levels of energy.

It's probably a good idea to confine your kitten to a single room in the beginning, at least for the first few days or so. This at least helps you to ensure that they are well-acquainted with the litter box, and for your kitten, helps him to adjust gradually to new surroundings. After all, he has just been separated from his mother, his siblings, and his old home, and thrust into a completely different home with relative strangers. Best to allow him to make the transition a little at a time - or one room at a time, anyway. Provide him with all he needs within this room. Meanwhile, if you haven't already, take a look at the rest of the house and try to see if you can spot any potential danger areas or zones you might want to address.

Here are a few things you might want to watch out for:

- Secure loose wires, loose cords or cables, and curtains or table cloths that reach all the way to the floor. Kittens seem to like playing with dangling things such as wires or threads and the like, but strong curtain cords, electrical cables, or any other loose wires should be off limits to these cats. You don't want them getting strangled accidentally, or worse, electrocuted should they even think of chewing on those wires.

- No breakables or dainty, precious pieces out in the open. And this goes for shelf spaces, too. Your Savannah cat will grow up sooner or later, and even as a kitten, it might already develop a propensity for jumping. And because this is a highly energetic breed with a penchant for playing, don't tempt them by leaving out breakable, valuable pieces out in the open.

- Secure dangerous, poisonous things around the home, such as poisonous plants, house cleaners or chemicals, medicines, pesticides.

- Aside from those dainty pieces, you might also want to secure heavy objects that may be liable of falling and possibly hitting your kitten with a thump.

- Store away small items such as small displays, toys, plastic bags, rubber bands, or other objects which he can possibly chew and swallow, and which might eventually lodge in his throat.

- Secure open containers of water, including toilet lids. Savannahs have a particular fondness of water, but that does not mean that all types of water are healthy or safe for them. You don't want them drowning in a tub full of water, an outdoor well, or even the toilet bowl - the latter of which cannot be sanitary. Exercise due caution.

- If your kitten has access to an open balcony or terrace, or a stairway, don't assume that he won't try to jump. Kittens don't have an inbuilt sense of safety, and Savannahs are, after all, great jumpers. Sure he may eventually grow up able to scale the highest point of your house, but as a kitten, that is not quite likely. You can probably use a wire netting or something similar to ensure he doesn't somehow slip through.

- A Savannah kitten will likely be underfoot many times, and will probably have the sense of adventure to explore the nooks and crannies of your home when you aren't looking. Look inside the washer and dryer before you turn it on. Be careful about opening and closing doors, before turning on the vacuum cleaner, lighting the fireplace, opening and closing the refrigerator, and even turning on or leaving a hot stove.

Chapter Four: Caring for Your New Savannah Cat

Bringing a Savannah kitten home can be the beginning of a new adventure for you and the rest of your household. It can sometimes be frustrating, maybe even exasperiating, but undertaken with the right attitude and the proper understanding of what a Savannah cat needs, it can be extremely rewarding.

The first thing you have to understand is that Savannah cats are, in some ways, different from most domestic cats. They are more energetic, for one thing, and they are not likely to want to lie around all day and sleep when they could be playing around with you instead. This can lead to what some might consider problem behaviors, but which are, in truth, simply the unique nature of Savannah cats that you must take into consideration when you bring one of these glamorous cats home. Making sure you know what is involved in caring for a Savannah, and making the appropriate household preparations, will ensure a better understanding between you and your new feline family member.

Habitat and Exercise Requirements for Savannah Cats

Savannah cats are not lap cats. They will not sit and purr quietly in your lap, even if they can fit comfortably on your lap. These are moderately to large cats, and many don't like being picked up or restrained in any way. They are quite affectionate, sometimes even dog-like in showing their loyalty, following you around the house, butting your legs with their head to signal their desire to play. The breed has excess energy to spare, and while their primary home should be indoors, they should also be allowed regular outdoors time, whether within a fenced enclosure or on a leash.

Some vertical space will be needed by the Savannah, as this breed is a great climber. Don't think in terms of how high they can climb, because they will pretty much reach the highest climbable point in your house - whether it is the shelves, the top of drawers and cabinets, or the fence keeping them in. Even if you watch them for a while and determine that "this fence he cannot climb" - consider his wild ancestry, his excess of energy, and his natural curiosity, persistence, and agility - and with enough time nothing is beyond his reach. So prepare your house accordingly. Clear the shelves above and below of precious and breakable things, and provide your Savannah cat a safe enclosure with a secure top out in your yard.

Because of its considerable energy levels, some form of daily exercise is required - whether it is in the form of walking (on a leash) or games and play. You will likely want to work in half an hour or so of walking and as much as that, or more, time for games. This breed loves interaction as much as it does physical exertion, especially if it means that he gets to demonstrate his playful, affectionate nature with you, his owner. Provide them with a wide assortment of safe toys (toys that he won't be able to swallow and thus cause an emergency crisis) to keep him occupied. You don't have to spend a lot of money for this - many household items like cardboard boxes, tennis balls, some chew toys, and a bunch of other simple items to mix it up should suffice. Be aware also that this cat has a fondness for water - and they will paw at shallow bowls of water, dip into aquariums, or sometimes even learn to open faucets and showers! Just be sure not to leave large and open containers of water around - especially tanks of water that are larger than your cat, unless you want them to risk the possibility of drowning.

Given their size and their natural activity levels, Savannah cats must be allowed sufficient running room inside the house. If you are not able to give them a room of their own - you must provide them ample space that would at least contain their sleeping area and bed, their food and water bowls, their litter box, some vertical space for climbing, and enough room for running around and playing. If you ensure that you afford them these basic things, chances are you'll keep them happy and content in their new home.

Toys and Accessories for Savannah Cats

You'll probably want to provide your Savannah cat with a wide selection of toys and accessories to begin with. Just remember to steer clear of breakables, toys with removable parts that are small enough to be swallowed, small foam balls, toys with strings or ribbons, or toys with any lead content. You'll probably discover that your cat will develop a certain fondness for one or two of these toys - each cat will prove individual and unique in this case - and after this fondness is spent, he will move on to other, new favorites. Such are cats. Some recommended toys include tennis balls, cardboard boxes, cat wands, crumpled paper, stuffed animals that are also chewable, and other similar toys.

You might also want to provide him with a suitable scratching post not only to spare your rugs and other furniture from his nails, but also to provide him with a handy way of stretching their spine and sharpening their (hopefully, regularly-trimmed) nails. And because these cats are great climbers, providing them with enough climbing perches and boxes to hide in should provide them an enjoyable habitat to play in.

The Savannah as an Indoor Cat

Most breeders and experts are in agreement regarding this one thing about Savannah cats: this is a breed that should not be allowed to roam freely outdoors. Because of the Savannah's natural curiosity, and their penchant to follow anything that attracts them, they are extremely high risk for meeting vehicular accidents. Not only that, Savannah cats are still relatively rare and expensive enough to be considered fair game for anyone with malicious intent looking to make a buck. Don't chance it. Experts say that cats kept mostly indoors have a considerably longer life span than those who are allowed to roam freely outdoors. These indoor cats are usually healthier, too - because they avoid the temptation of eating unhealthy things, being poisoned, being attacked by other animals, and being exposed to diseases or viruses from other cats and stray animals.

Chapter Five: Meeting Your Savannah Cat's Nutritional Needs

It can sometimes feel like feeding your cat should be a simple thing, but at the same time is the most complicated thing when you are faced with the wide variety of cat food available in the market. There is a wide range to choose from, and many claim themselves to be the best in the market for your cat. Recently, many people are turning the tables on commercial cat food companies, feeding their cats homemade food, which they claim is healthier. It goes without saying that Savannah owners must wonder if their hybrid cats require specialized nutrition or diet different from most domestic cats? This chapter contains an overview of some of the basics of feline nutrition, tips on how to choose high quality cat food brand, and various other tips and guidelines when it comes to feeding your Savannah cat.

The Nutritional Needs of Cats

You've probably come across the phrase, "Cats are obligate carnivores." But what does that really mean?

Think of any cat in the wild, and how they survive. What do they eat? Cats are predators, natural hunters, and the bulk of their diet in a natural environment usually consists of raw meat. Even now, many domestic cats hunt and eat mice, while many feral cats that live on the outskirts of human society mainly live on prey: mice, birds, and other small animals. Now think of what packaged cat food contains. The question to ask yourself now is whether they are getting the same nutrients that they need from cat food as they would be getting from their natural diet?

It is a legitimate question. We all know that we are what we eat - and this applies to humans as well as cats. Many instances of diseases and illnesses, in fact, can likely be traced back to poor diet and nutritional habits. We want to keep our cats healthy, so what do we feed them? Some owners have converted to raw meat and homemade diets, but this is not for everyone. For one thing, feeding them a steady diet of raw meat might actually make thing worse. How sure are you that you are not ignoring their other nutritional needs which they get from food other than meat? And for another thing, raw meat is a fertile breeding ground for bacteria, and unless you know what you're doing, you could actually make things worse for your cat. Consult with your veterinarian before undertaking such a drastic dietary change.

In many instances, perhaps all you need to do is to find the right kind or mix of cat food. In order to do this, the first thing you have to learn is what comprises a balanced feline nutritional diet.

Proteins

Cats derive their protein requirements mainly from meats rather than vegetables, as their digestive system might not be particularly suited to digesting too much fiber and grains. Proteins help build tissues, organs, and help in the production of antibodies and a healthy immune system.

Amino Acids

It is important that your cat's diet contain the essential amino acids that he needs because cats cannot synthesize them in quantities sufficient to meet his needs. Of the different amino acids such as methionine, leucine, tryptophan, lysine, valine, arginine, histidine, phenylalanine, and isoleucine, special mention needs to be made of taurine. Most Savannah breeders agree that compared to other cat breeds, Savannah cats seem to require more Taurine - which helps in fetal development and the prevention of heart and eye disease. Amino acids can mostly be derived from protein sources such as meats.

Fats

Fats are a concentrated energy source, and are also used by the body for the absorption of fat-soluble vitamins. They also help in digestion, provide protection for the internal organs, and gives the cat's body insulation.

Carbohydrates

Some carbohydrates are necessary for your cat as these help maintain the health of the intestines and also supply energy to some critical organs. But please remember that high fiber sources are not good for all cats, especially kittens. Good fiber sources for cats must be moderately fermentable.

Vitamins and Minerals

Many vitamins and minerals that are necessary in a cat's diet should also be supplied in their diet because cats cannot synthesize them in their bodies. These help maintain a cat's metabolism, bone and teeth health, among others. Please remember that it is never a good idea to provide your cat with vitamin and mineral supplements unless specifically prescribed and approved by your veterinarian.

Water

Like most mammals, cats need water to survive. Keeping them properly hydrated by providing them with a ready supply of clean drinking water can actually keep many illnesses at bay.

How to Select a High-Quality Cat Food Brand

The selection of high-quality cat food should not be based on advertisements or commercials, but on what you see on the label of the product itself. It is important, therefore, that you learn to read the label and ingredients list of a packaged cat food, to determine which is better than others. Below are a few tips to guide you as you search your way down that aisle:

- Look for age-appropriate cat food. You won't feed the same food to a kitten as you will to a senior cat, or to an adult cat. These differences have to do with the specific nutritional needs of the cat in these various life stages. Growing cats need different nutrition compared to adult cats or cats that are past their prime. This is also called the nutritional adequacy statement.

- Look at the label. What is the cat food called? Avoid those calling the cat food various labels such as "meal," or "dinner," or "formula" These labels are usually applied for foods that contain more than 25%, but less than 95% of the main ingredient. Opt for simpler labels, such as "tuna cat food," or "chicken cat food." Apparently, manufacturers can only do this if the product contains at least 95% of the ingredient named, which means you are at least assured that you are getting a meatier product. Avoid qualifiers such as "with," and "and." Prefixing other ingredients with these qualifiers may make you think that you are getting more quality for you money, but the truth is that these add-ons can mean as little as 3%, while it also allows them to decrease the first ingredient to lower than 95%, as long as the two stated ingredients add up to at least 95%.

- Next, look at the ingredients list. Remember when we said that cats are obligate carnivores? This means that the primary ingredient of the cat food must be quality meat such as chicken, lamb, beef, etc. Always look at the first few ingredients, as manufacturers are legally required to list ingredients in descending order based on weight. In short, the product contains more of the ingredients that are listed first. These should primarily be meat-based.

- If you are not sure whether dry or canned cat food is better, you might want to try a mixture of the two. It seems that historically, cats derive most of their water from the food that they eat - and even until now, they don't really have a reliable sense of thirst. Make sure that they stay properly hydrated by including some water content in the meal itself, which means canned food. On the other hand, dry food keeps better, and can even be left freely in the bowl for the cat to eat whenever he gets hungry. Mixing up your options can provide some variety to your cat, as you may find him getting bored of the usual fare after too long. In fact, it's probably good idea to have a ready list of good cat food brands just in case your cat begins hankering for something new.

- Good sources of carbohydrates include brown rice, barley, oats, and other whole grains. Avoid, as much as possible, corn meal, corn meal gluten, and wheat gluten. These are cheap fillers and may actually be harmful to your cat.

Don't forget that ultimately, the best judge of which cat food is better is your cat. Try to notice if your cat shows any signs of change - whether for the good or for the bad - whenever you change their regular diet. Remember not to make any drastic dietary changes without your veterinarian's approval, and always give your cats time to adjust to new food by gradually in order to give them a chance to adjust.

Dangerous Foods to Avoid

TICA has advised that feeding Savannah cats are not unlike how you would feed most cats - and it is really your choice whether you opt for dry, canned, or a raw meat diet for your Savannah. Just make sure that this is an informed decision on your part - and that you are undertaking any dietary changes with the full approval of your veterinarian. This is important because your cat's unique health conditions may not warrant such changes as you would like to make, or it may interfere with medications he may currently be on. This also applies to your decision on how to feed your cat - whether free feeding or based on a regular schedule. Many times, it really depends on your unique situation.

Just remember that not all foods are safe - and some human foods can actually be lethal for felines. Below are some human foods that are actually dangerous for cats. Take note of them, and make sure that none are within easy reach of your cat.

- Alcohol
- Candy and Gum
- Chives
- Chocolate
- Coffee
- Dairy Products
- Energy Drinks
- Fat Trimmings and Bones
- Garlic
- Grapes and Raisins
- Mushrooms
- Mustard seeds
- Onions/leeks
- Peach pits
- Potato leaves/stems
- Raw Eggs
- Rhubarb leaves
- Tea
- Tomato leaves/stems
- Walnuts
- Xylitol
- Yeast dough

If your Savannah cat eats any of these foods, contact the Pet Poison Control hotline right away at (888) 426 – 4435.

Chapter Six: Training Your Savannah Cat

    The Savannah cat is not a cat for everyone, especially not for first time cat owners. Even some of the more experienced feline lovers will find that living with a Savannah presents them with some unique and interesting challenges. Highly intelligent and with great energy and motivation for play, Savannahs need a lot of attention. While extremely loving and loyal, this is a high energy and playful breed whose natural propensity for games and demands for attention can quickly turn destructive if not trained properly early on. If you don't have the time, energy or the patience to socialize and play regularly with your Savannah, then this is probably not the cat for you.

That said, being able to interact and bond regularly with your Savannah, nurturing his natural instincts while keeping his behavior under control can be a most rewarding and worthwhile experience. In this chapter, we look at some of the basics of training for your Savannah, including socialization, litter training, tricks training, and addressing potential problem behaviors.

Socializing Your New Kitten

Proper socialization is a must, and is likely what will ensure the health and survival of the kitten. Like most babies, kittens pretty much absorb what they need to know to survive during the first few weeks of their life - learning from their mother, their littermates, and you. They learn how to cover their pee and poo from their mother, they learn how to restrain their hunger impulses once the mother no longer feeds them whenever they want, they learn how to deal with other cats such as their mother and their siblings - and what it means to restrain themselves from too much biting and scratching in play, and most of all, they learn how to deal with humans and most of strange things they will find in the human world.

Raising a properly socialized kitten means that your cat is less likely to grow up scared and frightened by each new stranger it meets, or each new sight, sound and smell she is exposed to. Can you imagine the stressful life a cat must lead if it tends to jump in fear at every sound? Now imagine how many strange sounds a cat will find in your home alone - TV, radio, furniture moving around, phone ringing, appliances going off, children running around. A well-adjusted cat begins as a properly socialized kitten, which simply means that he was exposed to a number of things early on in his life within a positive situation so that he learns not to perceive everything strange and new as a threat.

They key to socialization is not to rush things. First of all, a kitten should not be taken away from its mother before it is ready. It may be fully weaned, but is it ready for complete separation with everything it has known since then? Some kittens also do experience separation anxiety. Previously, breeders considered the age of separation to be at around 8 weeks, when the kittens were fully weaned. More recently, however, some breeders were prolonging the separation age from 10 to 12 weeks. It isn't just about the readiness to be separated from its source of milk. It's also about how ready a cat is to be separated - which mostly depends on how its first human socialization experience has proceeded until then. It has been said that a cat's crucial time for socialization experience happens within the first 7-8 weeks of its life, though there is still a window that extends up until it reaches 7 months. Ideally, however, those first few weeks has been packed full of caring and nurturing from both you and its mother, lots of interactive play with other kittens, and enough human handling so that it no longer considers humans as a threat.

When you bring your kitten home for the first time, make sure to provide them a proper place in the house. Keep them confined in one room, to begin with, and within that room, provide them with enough toys, hiding places and various odds and ends so that it doesn't feel isolated in its confinement. Rugs, small boxes to serve as a den, an assortment of toys, and possibly a radio to filter in the occasional sounds, can serve as a primary introduction into its life with you.

Be sure to interact with them often - at least daily, but ideally more than once during a day. You have to feed them anyway, right? Give them a pet and a loving hug while you're at it, too. It may not seem like much, but it is a way for you to introduce yourselves to each other, make them feel at home, and also a continuation of the process of their socialization.

Gradually, begin to introduce him to the other members of your family. Though make sure that he has the proper vaccinations before you expose him to other cats, dogs, or other pet members in your household. Consult with your veterinarian to determine when it is safe to do so.

Don't forget that play is very important to a Savannah kitten - and something that they will probably never grow out of. They enjoy playing, and thus is one very good way of socializing and bonding with them. Aside from teaching them the limits of what they can and cannot do in terms of biting and scratching, play also offers them a way to work off their high level of energy. If they don't have such an outlet, this may lead to destructive behavior later on.

Savannahs are slow to mature, which they usually do when they reach three years. By then, they could go to be quite sizeable cats. There are some owners who also make it a habit of taking their cats out for a walk, and a Savannah would fit a leash and harness beautifully - provided, of course, that he has been given time enough to get used to it. You will need lots of room in the house and in the backyard if you plan to keep a Savannah as a pet. So while it is a good idea to fence in the yard, you could practice him for short walks on a leash out in the yard in the beginning. Later on, with your veterinarian's consent, and when you feel the cat is ready, you can begin taking him out for longer walks outside. In this way, his exposure to other places, other humans, and other dogs and cats, is supervised by you. As always, make this a positive experience for your cat, as he begins to develop his self-confidence and satisfies his natural curiosity in a safe and nurturing way.

It is not really wise to leave him to wander around like most domestic cats - regardless of whether your yard is fenced in or not. Savannahs are known to be great climbers, and some are even intelligent enough to open doors and windows. You don't want him getting loose and climbing over the fence - so unless you are pretty certain of your fence, you should not leave your Savannah cat outside in the yard unsupervised, or without a leash. Savannah cats have a strong hunting instinct, and can literally follow their mark indefinitely. They are also extremely curious and highly energetic. Add to that the usual dangers of vehicles and roads, Savannahs and the outside human world simply do not mix.

These are only rational precautions - in no time, that kitten will grow up to be a sexually mature adult, and you can never tell the degree to which it has inherited its Serval ancestor's wilder instincts. Discipline, and the limits of what he can and cannot do should be established in the beginning, during this important period of learning. Many Savannah owners come to realize later on that their cats can sometimes begin behaving out of control and they can no longer rein the cats in, and they wonder what went wrong. Invest enough time, energy, patience, and training early on during the kitten's life, and you'll have a valuable Savannah to keep for the rest of its life.

Litter Training for Kittens

One of the reasons why a kitten shouldn't be taken from its mother before it is ready is because kittens basically learn all that they need to know about using a litter from their mother. They emulate what they see their mother do - peeing in the box and then covering it up. Once you bring them home, half of the work should already be done. What you need to do is to make sure that this habit continues.

Below are a few tips in litter training your kitten once he comes home:

- Make sure that he is acquainted with the box. Some owners like to place him in the box directly after eating. Do this several days in a row until he gets it. He usually will get it easier than you think.
- For the first few days, keep him in a confined room that also contains the litter box. This limits his access and choices of a variety of other spots in which he can do the deed.
- Make sure that the litter box is located in a suitable spot. Don't put it near his food and water bowls, for

one thing. And don't place it somewhere that is likely to be disturbed by appliances, people, or other pets. Ideally, it should be somewhere that is easily accessible by your cat, and that is at least semi-private, but not too private that it becomes difficult for you to reach and clean regularly.

- Scoop regularly. Cats are naturally fastidious creatures, and they won't appreciate having to go in an already dirty litterbox. It's akin to humans not wanting to use a dirty toilet. It makes more work for you, but it is all part and parcel of keeping a pet in the house.

- Sometimes, cats not using the litterbox is simply a quirk of the individual cat. Vary it up, read up on what works for others, and try it out yourself. Some have reported that their cats don't like peeing and pooping in the same box, so they keep two litterboxes for their cats. Others have reported a dislike of cats sharing litter boxes with other cats, so if you keep other cats in the house, this may be it. Quite possibly, the dislike of using the litterbox may be the result of some power or dominance play between two or more cats inside the house. Sometimes, it can even be the result of an illness or condition of the bowels, and a visit to the veterinarian is in order. Or it could be the result of a changing preference in the type of litter you use. Be observant of your cat's behavior, read up, and experiment to find what works for you.

- Sometimes, what isn't working probably isn't the litterbox or litterbox habits. Some cats that feel stressed act out by not using the litter box. Look at your family's routine and how your cat is coping. Maybe he's feeling a bit stressed out or harrassed by too many changes happening within his human family.

Dealing with Problem Behaviors

If you have decided to live with a Savannah, there are a few quirks of this breed that are a given, and that should be considered when you bring them home. In domestic cats, these might be considered destructive behavior, but they are simply natural for the Savannah - given his high energy and wild heritage. Managing these sorts of behavioral problems probably means that you will have to adjust your lifestyle to meet their unique needs. If what you are looking for is a quiet, tame, and domestic lap cat, then the Savannah cat is probably not right for you. This lovely breed needs an owner who will fully understand, accept, and know how to manage their unique quirks and traits.

- Leaving breakables out in the open is a huge no-no for a home with a Savannah. And it doesn't matter how high up on the shelf you store those precious objects. These cats are climbers, and they will climb closets, shelves, trees and other high places, many times knocking over stuff to do so.

- You have to have a sense of humor when dealing with these cats. Some will hide up on a shelf and then drop things down on you when you're not looking. Others have reported their Savannahs having a penchant of hiding when they're near, and then pouncing on them to scare them. They like to play, and sometimes, they won't take no for an answer. This breed needs a lot of interaction, and the lack of an active playmate inside the home might instead lead them to some destructive behavior.

- In addition to the above, this is not a breed that you can leave alone in the house for too long. What with their need for attention, interactive game play, and their Houdini-like tactics, you might find yourself dealing with a Savannah with some behavioral problems. You need to have the time and energy to devote to this breed, because this is a cat will act out, and won't respond to obvious signs of displeasure simply to please you.

- There have also been reports of aggressive Savannahs that spit, hiss, and even attack people. On the one hand, this can probably be traced back to their wild Serval heritage, and the degree to which it manifests in Savannahs may be affected by how far removed the cat is from its wild Serval ancestor. This is why breeders are actively trying to breed down among purebred Savannahs, and outcrossing is no longer permitted. If this is your first time to bring a Savannah home, opt for a later generation, ideally F4, F5 or later. On the other hand, such behavior manifesting may simply be a result of improper socialization skills when they were kittens, and not enough continuing socialization afterwards. This is why it is important to get your cat from a reputable breeder, and why prospective Savannah owners should realize how much work this cat can be. One has to be willing to put in the work for this breed, and unless you are ready, willing and able to do so, then this is probably not the breed for you.

Chapter Seven: Grooming Your Savannah Cat

Savannah cats are generally low maintenance when it comes to grooming. But while no more than weekly grooming sessions might be needed, it is always a good idea to make each grooming session a positive experience for your Savannah. Not only does it keep him clean, healthy and presentable, but positive, regular grooming sessions with you can be a wonderful bonding and socialization experience for you and your cat.

Tips for Bathing and Grooming Savannah Cats

The Savannah has a coat that is fairly low maintenance, with a short, soft coat that requires no more than a weekly brushing. Savannahs do shed, but making coat grooming and brushing a regular thing will easily keep the likelihod of shed hair around your house under control. Remember to be gentle - especially around the belly and chest areas. Other than that, the Savannah, like most fastidious cats, will pretty much take care of itself. This is also a good time for you to make a physical examination of your cat's body. Run your hands lightly around his legs, torso, neck, and back, and make sure that there aren't any abnormal lumps or swellings or other possible signs of illness or disease.

Neither will you have to bathe your cat, although some owners do begin building this habit in their kittens early on. Most of those who show their Savannahs want their cat to get used to the idea of bathing, and doing it early on during the cat's life will - even if he never becomes fond of it, will at least teach him to tolerate it.

Savannahs do love water, and this might make some people think that they would also love having a bath. Not necessarily - there is a big difference between liking water and being forced to submit to a bath. The Savannah's ancestor, the wild Serval, regularly hunted for frogs and small fish in water, and it is likely that your Savannah may have inherited this love of water. Bathing a Savannah may not be necessary, but if you do want to be able to build the habit in them, start them out when they are young. Use qualiy shampoo, and be thorough in rinsing off the shampoo from their coat. When you are only beginning, keep bath times short, and if she wants to escape from the bath, let her, and try again another time. Nothing will put a kitten off bathing more than memories of unfavorable experiences regarding the bath.

If you are one of those people, on the other hand, who are completely happy to stick to regular brushing, you might want to add some kitten wipes to your arsenal of grooming tools for cleaning the corners of your cat's eyes, their nose, and their muzzle.

Other Grooming Tasks

There are other tasks to complete your Savannah's weekly grooming, and like with coat grooming, these are also pretty straightforward. Though you might want to pay particularly close attention to your Savannah's tall ears, but aside from some extra care, cleaning their ears is not that different from how you would clean the ears of most cats.

Other grooming tasks include trimming your Savannah's nails, cleaning his ears, and brushing his teeth.

Trimming Your Cat's Nails

A cat's claws can be extra sharp - particularly if your Savannah makes a regular habit of sharpening her claws. While there are some owners out there who prefer to de-claw their cat, it is generally considered more humane to simply trim their claws. Doing so weekly is a good practice.

Many cats, however, don't like it when you touch their paws, and attempting to trim their claws when they aren't used to it might cause those claws to come out! If this is your first time at trimming your cat's claws - and your cat's first time - you might want to spend a week or more just getting her used to the feeling of having her paws handled by you. You can try pressing gently on their foot to cause her to extend their claws, just to get her used to the feel of it. When you feel that you are both ready, press the paws until the claws are extended, and just snip! Use quality cat nail trimmers to do this, as using regular human nail trimmers will not work. Be conservative in the amount of nail you trim. There is a blood vessel beneath the nails that provides its blood supply, and if you aren't careful, you might end up cutting this, too.

If you aren't sure about what to do, or are nervous about wielding the nail clippers yourself, have a professional groomer or vet show you how it's done before attempting it yourself.

Cleaning Your Cat's Ears

A Savannah's ears are one of their outstanding features, and the tall pair of ears standing tall and upright also contribute to their wild look. But ears can also be a breeding ground of ear mites and other bacteria which can cause infections, so cleaning their ears is also important. But because of the sensitivity of a cat's ears - particularly inside the ear - always remember to be gentle and careful when cleaning.

A healthy ear should be clean, with no debris, no odor, and minimal if little earwax visible. Use a moistened cotton ball or a pieze of gauze (never use q-tips!) to clean inside your cat's ears, gently wiping away any dirt or debris you find in there. Don't go too deep, or you might injure her. If you detect any bad smell or odor coming from inside their ears, then bring her immediately to a veterinarian.

Brushing Your Cat's Teeth

It may seem strange to think of brusing a cat's teeth, but cats also do suffer from some dental and oral problems like gingivitis, periodontitis, and other conditions that can affect the health of their teeth, tongue, and gums. Providing them a good chew toy can help, but it is always a good idea to build the habit of brushing their teeth early on.

Always remember to use toothbrush and toothpaste that are especially designed for cats. Using human toothpaste, for instance, is not a good idea as these contains substances that may be harmful to cats.

If you are brushing your cat's teeth for the first time, it is recommended that you first get him used to the feeling of a foreign object rubbing against his teeth. Some people may use their fingers, others use a cotton swab. Go slowly, touching only the front teeth at first by gently pushing back their lips. Use the cotton swab to gently rub it against their front teeth. Next, try dabbing some of the toothpaste on their lips. After some time, you can try applying this to your cat's teeth using the cotton swab at first, and maybe later on using a cat tootbrush.

Be patient. You might not be completely successful at first, and you'll find yourself dealing with a squirmy patient. Don't force it on your cat or you'll find him hiding from you whenever he sees you holding the toothpaste tube. Like in all matters of grooming, make it a positive experience as much as possible. With time, your Savannah will get used to it, and probably even enjoy it.

Chapter Eight: Breeding Your Savannah Cat

First of all, you should ask yourself why you want to breed Savannah cats. If it is solely for the money - which may be tempting to some given how expensive this breed is - then this venture is probably not for you. Breeding Savannah cats requires time, persistence, and a complete dedication to the development of this breed. Money itself would not be enough of a motivation to see you through the difficulties, frustrations, and years of learning that you have before you.

If, on the other hand, you are not interested in the money, and want to breed your Savannah simply because you want to have their kittens, the same warnings apply. Savannahs are expensive because so much goes into their breeding and development, and unless you have the proper TICA registration papers for your litter, you might have difficulty finding homes for kittens that are not registered. Already there is a growing number of unwanted Savannahs out there, whether from unregistered breeders who did not know what to do with the kittens, or from owners who discovered that they no longer had the capacity to care for these energetic and lively cats.

If you are seriously considering becoming a full-pledged Savannah breeder, then read on. This chapter gives a general overview of what to expect in the field of Savannah cat breeding.

What It Means to Breed Savannah Cats

It is important to remember that it is not legal to own Savannah cats in some states in the United States. Certain states restrict ownership of Savannahs, while others consider it illegal to do so. So the first thing you should do is check out the legality of owning Savannahs in your area. If it is illegal where you live, that pretty much decides it for you, unless you have it in mind to move. Even if it isn't illegal, it is important to know which states restict or forbid ownership, given that you will one day be finding homes for the kittens. Breeding responsibly means taking care of your kittens from birth until they find new and loving homes.

Savannah cats are a relatively new breed, and they were only accepted for Championship Status by TICA in 2012. TICA is the only cat organization in the world that recognizes and accepts this hybrid breed, and even now, Savannahs can only be shown in the Advanced New Breed category because there are, as yet, not enough registered cats to warrant showing in the Championship category.

And because this breed is, in many ways, still not firmly established, breeders can get pretty technical when it comes to Savannah breeding lingo and expertise. Below you will find some of the more common terminologies you will come across sooner or later when you are dealing with Savannah cats, followed by some of the difficulties inherent in Savannah cat breeding.

Filial Generation: (F1, F2, F3, etc.)

"Filial" refers to family generation, and this is reckoned from how far away an offspring is from its Serval ancestor. The offspring of a Serval and a domestic cat is referred to as "F1" - as in the case of the original Savannah cat produced by the crossbreeding of an African Serval and a domestic Siamese cat.

An F2 generation has the Serval for a grandparent, or is two generations away. An F3 has a great grandparent who is a Serval, and so on. The filial generation reckoned by numbers tells you how far away a Savannah is down the line from a wild African Serval cat.

"A-Registered", "B-Registered," "C-Registered" or "SBT"

Savannahs are also distinguised based on their level of Savannah breeding - which is what the TICA uses for the registration of Savannah cats. The above are the Registration Codes that TICA uses in its Feline Registry.

For instance, "A-Registered Savannahs" are those with one Savannah parent - usually the result of an outcross with one of the permissible outcross breeds - e.g., a Savannah and a Domestic Shorthair.

"B-Registered Savannahs" mean that the cat has two Savannah parents, but not all grandparents are Savannahs. So if you cross two "A-Registered" Savannahs, or if you cross one "A-Registered Savannah" and one "B-Registered Savannah, you will get a "B-Registered Savannah" because even if both parents are Savannahs, the cat still has one outcross grandparent.

"C-Registered Savannahs" mean that both parents and all four grandparents are Savannahs. "C-Registered" Savannahs are the result of two generations of Savannah to Savannah breeding, with no outcrosses in those two generations. Crossing two "B-Registered," or crossing one

"B-Registered" and one "C-Registered" Savannah will result in a "C-Registered" Savannah.

"SBT," which stands for "Stud Book Traditional," means that the Savannah is the result of three generations of Savannah-to-Savannah breeding. Crossing two "C-Registered" Savannahs will result in an SBT, and they are what the TICA considers "purebred" Savannahs. Any serious Savannah cat breeder should aim for the production of SBT Savannahs, and as more SBT cats are bred, it is hoped the Savannahs will become more established as a breed.

Difficulties Inherent in Savannah Cat Breeding

There are a few inherent difficulties in Savannah cat breeding, and it takes patience, dedication, and a good working knowledge of feline crossbreeding to hurdle these difficulties. The list below is by no means exhaustive, neither is it certain in all instances and situations. But they should put prospective breeders on the alert as to the roadblocks that may lie ahead of them as they seek to contribute in the development of the Savannah cat breed.

- Savannah cat ownership is restricted in some states in the United States, and illegal in others. You need to do your background check on local ordinances and laws governing the legality of wild or domesticated hybrid crosses in your area, and definitely regarding licensing laws before you even consider starting a breeding program. Outside of the United States, Canada has certain restrictions on the ownership of F1 and F2 generations, and special permits are required for importing these cats from the United States. In Australia, importation of the Savannah cat is banned.

- While you are essentially "breeding down" a wild cat - keeping their wild appearance as much as possible while retaining the temperaments of more domestic cats, you cannot completely get rid of their wild nature. These are energetic cats, great jumpers and climbers, and there have been reports of some Savannahs intelligent enough to open drawers, closet doors, and even windows. They will spray to mark their territory, and some have even been reported to hunt local wildlife and other smaller pets in the nearby areas. You need a good and secure area for a cattery, and you will need to be able to maintain some semblance of discipline among the Savannahs you will be housing. Traits of the wild Serval are usually more pronounced among the earlier Savannah generations. Daily, regular and constant socialization and supervision is a must to prevent them from reverting to the wild. It goes without saying that cruelty, neglect and abandonment are not options once you discover that these cats are a handful for you - better know what you're getting into before bringing one of these cats home, or before you start a breeding program.

- Male fertility seems to be a problem among the earlier generations of Savannahs - one of the more common manifestations of hybrid inviability. Male Savannahs are usually sterile until the fifth generation and later, and even F5 males are usually smaller than the females, which makes breeding difficult. Recently, sterile male Savannahs have also appeared in F5 to F6 generations. You will usually have to breed fertile F5 or later generation males to earlier generations of females - all of which are usually fertile. And because earlier generation females are usually larger in size than their male counterparts, this also provides some difficulties in the actual breeding process.

- In order to retain the desirable characteristics of the "purebred" Savannah - you will have to be selective about the cats you breed. Remember that what you are aiming for are the clear, spotted coat patterns and other physical characteristics set out in the TICA Breed Standard, but with a friendly temperament that is closer to its domestic, rather than its wild, ancestry. In order to achieve this desirable traits, outcrosses were permitted to selected breeds, including: Oriental Shorthairs, Egyptian Maus, Ocicat, and the Domestic Shorthair. TICA considers the following as "impermissible" outcrosses: Bengal and Maine Coon cats. These days, however, outcrossing is seldom used as there are now enough male Savannah studs available. Regardless, however, you still have to aim to breed for the desirable traits, avoiding genetic illnesses and genetic and temperamental "flaws" as much as possible.

- Pregnancies that result from crossbreeding are often difficult. Because of the differences in size between the parents (even among Savannah-to-Savannah breeding, where the sizes can vary greatly even in one litter), and the difference in gestation period between domestic cats and Servals, some kittens may be born prematurely and then require round-the-clock care. In some instances, pregnancies are either aborted or absorbed.

- Serval females are picky about their mates, and this characteristic also seems to appear in the earlier generations of Savannah females - which are usually larger compared to later generations. While crossbreeding does happen, even among hybrid Savannahs, it may be quite difficult to produce a successful mating or breeding between a larger female Savannah and a smaller male Savannah or smaller male domestic cat, especially when the female is uncooperative.

- While Savannahs are a generally healthy breed, some diseases have manifested in certain cats, such as

Hypertrophic Cardiomyopathy (HCM) and PK Deficiency. On the other hand, some Savannahs have been found to inherit the Serval tendency to have smaller livers, though the medical effect of this has not yet been established. Some breeders are wary about the use of the anesthetic ketamine, and about the use of live modified vaccines on Servals - though many veterinarians see no scientific basis for this alarm. The fact is is that this breed is still too new for any breed-specific health conditions to be established. Breeders should therefore be aware of any diseases which the Savannah's ancestry - both wild and domestic - may have, be updated regarding any health news in the Savannah breeding field, and bringing their cats for regular veterinary and health checks is a must.

As a final word, you should seek registration with TICA as a Savannah cat breeder if you are really serious about breeding these gorgeous cats. You will generally be required to sign the TICA Code of Ethics, submit the required forms and pay the requisite fees, and be familiar with the By-laws, Registration Rules, Show Rules and Standing Laws of TICA. This registration needs to be renewed annually. Active membership and participation can provide the breeder with an extensive network of fellow breeders and Savannah cat enthusiasts to network with, exchange ideas with, have a discussion or conversation with, and just to share their love for and commitment to the development of the Savannah breed.

Basic Cat Breeding Information

Breeding Savannahs is generally no different from breeding most cats, except for a few crucial provisos:

- Breeding a larger Savannah with a domestic cat can be difficult - not only because of their size differences, but also because of the difference in their instinctive temperaments. In some instances, some female Savannahs will not willingly mate with a domestic cat - their female Serval ancestor usually chooses her mate in the wild. In other instances, breeding a Savannah and a smaller domestic cat can actually result in the injury, and sometimes even the death, of the smaller domestic cat. Keep in mind that when you are breeding cats with wild ancestry, constant supervision is necessary when they are brought together with other smaller pets and animals.
- Secondly, the gestation period between a domestic cat and a wild cat is different, which can make for a difficult pregnancy. 65 days is the average gestation period for a domestic cat, while it is 75 days for a

Serval. When you cross the two, or cross any of their offspring, some of the difficulties involved include pregnancies that are absorbed, aborted, or kittens that are born prematurely.

- It is generally advised that a prospective Savannah cat breeder begin with Savannah cats as their foundation breed. The original ancestors of the Savannah included the wild African Serval, but unless you have the knowledge, the capacity and the experience in dealing with wild cats, bringing one into your cattery is not recommended. Nor is crossing your Savannah with another hybrid wild cat such as the Bengal. If you really want to breed Savannahs, breed from the many later generations of Savannahs that have been produced. The TICA-stated goal is to achieve purebred Savannahs which are the result of at least three generations of Savannah to Savannah breeding.

Despite all the above-noted possible difficulties, Savannah breeding proceeds along the same general lines as the breeding process of most other breeds. Regardless of whether or not you aim to breed your Savannah, one of the first things you should be familiar with is the feline heat cycle. If you don't intend to breed your cat, then do the responsible thing and have him or her neutered. Doing so before they reach puberty or sexual maturity will not only reduce the risk of mammary cancer among the females, it will also prevent some of the more aggressive, sex-related behaviors such as yowling (calling), and among males - spraying or marking territory, and aggression.

The Feline Heat Cycle

In general, female cats reach their age of first heat at around 6 months, sometimes earlier at about 4-5 months. Male cats become sexually mature at around the same time, or about 5-7 months. Most breeders, however, do not recommend mating or breeding a cat at their age of first heat, but 18-24 months old or later, if possible. It is always advisable to wait until the cat has enough maturity and is fully grown before she bears the responsibility and stress of pregnancy and motherhood. In the meantime, it is incumbent upon the breeder to control or manage the female's heat cycles.

Cats are seasonally polyestrous, which means that they can be in heat several times during a year. And since males are typically attracted to a female cat in heat, unintentional or accidental matings may occur - which you don't want to happen, especially for a wild hybrid breed like the Savannah, unless you are willing to take responsibility for her kittens. A female cat can mate with multiple males while in heat, and because they are induced ovulators, they can produce a litter that has been sired by different cats, which is also known as superfecundity. It is estimated that a single cat can produce two to three litters per year, or up to 150 kittens in their breeding span of about ten years. This is why it is essential to know how to manage a female cat in heat. Not only will multiple pregnancies and births task the health of your queen, there is also the problem of the kittens and finding homes for all of them. Cat overpopulation is already a global problem. Some breeders choose to alternate breeding every two or three heat cycles, and then having the queen spayed when she reaches 5-6 years of age.

Be discerning in your selection of the queen and stud - not only should they be perfectly healthy and of the proper age, but you should also make your selection based on the ideal temperament of the kittens you are breeding. Many Savannah cats still do retain some of the wilder instincts of their Serval ancestors, which makes them difficult to care for especially when they grow old.

A cat's heat cycle moves in stages, the first of which is proestrus, which can last from 1-2 days, or sometimes even less. During proestrus, she will be "calling," and while she will not be willing to mate just yet, she will show some distinctive behaviors such as rolling around on the floor, licking her genitals, rubbing against your legs or against furniture, and she will have a propensity to try to escape the house in her attempts to find a mate.

During the second stage, or estrus, the queen will be ready to mate. It is advisable to keep your stud and queen together during this time to allow for repeated or multiple matings and a successful pregnancy. Chances are, she will get pregnant from the later matings, after she has already been induced to ovulate. You don't want another tomcat sneaking in in the meantime and fathering a few kittens. On the average, estrus can last for about a week, though sometimes for a shorter or longer period depending on the cat.

A female cat that has not been bred during estrus will enter the interestrus stage, which lasts for about a week, after which she will again start her cycle, entering the proestrus and estrus stages once more. If a queen has not been bred for successive heat cycles, then her cycles will become longer and more frequent. It is generally not advisable to allow three heat cycles to go by without breeding, so breeders usually seek to manage their cat's cycle in various ways. Consult your veterinarian for help in managing your queen's heat cycle.

If your cat was bred and ovulated, but she did not become pregnant, she enters metestrus, during which she will not show any signs of reproductive activity or about 5-7 weeks. If, on the other hand, the breeding was successful, she will enter a gestation period lasting for an average of 65-77 days. If the queen aborts or loses her kittens for whatever reason, she will once again resume her cycle after about 2-3 weeks.

Pregnancy and Queening

A pregnant or nursing mother is referred to as queen, and the process of birthing is referred to as queening. Some of the signs of a pregnant queen are nipples that are enlarged and more pink, weight gain, and a noticeable increase in appetite. You probably won't be able to tell that your cat is pregnant until she is sometime in her third week of pregnancy, which can be confirmed by a veterinarian. Around two weeks before she is due, you'll find her becoming more affectionate, and definite signs of nesting behavior such as seeking out solitary or private areas. Consult with your veterinarian regarding dietary changes, but in general, it is advisable to gradually increase your cat's diet during the final weeks of gestation until she is eating about 25% of her usual diet. This increased food intake will have to be kept up until after she has given birth and is lactating, to help her produce enough milk as she nurses her kittens.

Cats in general including Savannah cats, don't usually require much assistance during the birthing process, or during queening. What you can do is prepare a nesting box for her that should be large enough to contain both the mother and her kittens. This should be placed in a private room that is not often disturbed by pet or human traffic, or other loud noises or sounds. You should introduce her to this box, get her comfortable with it for the few weeks before she is due, and chances are she will give birth in that nesting box. Though be prepared for the possibility that she might want to sneak off somewhere when you aren't looking and have her kittens somewhere more secret. Sometimes, she'll probably surprise you one morning when you wake up and she has already given birth to her litter. Follow her and make sure that her choice of a birthing site is safe and secure, moving the kittens to the box if possible, with as little time as you can manage spent holding each kitten. Too much human handling early on may cause the mother to reject a kitten. If she was amenable enough to have her litter in the box you provided, be sure you are there with her when she does give birth, ready to provide assistance should it be necessary. Have the number of your vet and local emergency services on hand in case there is trouble, and if this is your first time, it is always advisable to have an experienced breeder with you to help and guide you through the process. In general, though, most cats will give birth without any help, their instincts kicking in quite strongly even for first time mothers.

The average size of a Savannah litter is variable, though it can range anywhere from 1 to 5 kittens. Their size will also vary, depending on the generation. Sometimes kittens of the same litter will also vary in size. Much of these details will depend on the breeding program you are adopting, and which Savannah generation you are breeding.

Make sure that the queen is nursing all her kittens. Some breeders advise leaving the kittens alone to bond with the queen for at least the first two days. Just ensure that they are kept warm and away from cold spots or chills. After this, it is time to gradually begin the process of socialization - even if it is only just regular momentary handling of the kittens in the beginning. Be gentle and careful in handling the kittens, and try to maintain the same level of attention and care for the pregnant queen as she nurses her kittens. Consult with your veterinarian regarding the best dietary plan for your new mother.

Raising and Weaning Kittens

TICA has advised that there is no real need to treat Savannahs differently than domestic cats when it comes to the food they eat, and most can be weaned the same way, too - through a gradual transition to moistened cat food until they no longer need to nurse from their mother. Some recommend using the kitten food you are aiming to feed them later on, moistened with formula.

Weaning usually begins at about 4 weeks, when the kittens start trying to eat their mother's food. Normally, the mother will push away the kittens. To begin the weaning process, you can try smearing the formula around the kittens' mouths at first, which they will eventually lick off. Once they have gotten used to the taste of the food, you can begin providing this to them in bowls. At the same time that you are gradually increasing the food intake of the kittens, you can also begin decreasing their mother's food intake to help her milk dry up naturally.

In general, most kittens are fully weaned by around 8-12 weeks, but this can be variable, and some Savannah kittens might require a longer period of time before they are fully weaned and ready to be separated from their mother. Don't rush it. As much as possible, kittens should not be rushed or forced or it might lead to potentially destructive behavior later on.

Chapter Nine: Showing Your Savannah Cat

If you are thinking of or planning on joining or entering your Savannah cat in a show, then this chapter is for you. At present, there is only one cat organization that registers Savannah cats - and that is the same organization which has figured so prominently in the history of this new breed's recognition and acceptance. The International Cat Association, or TICA, is currently the only cat organization that recognizes the Savannah cat breed, which they have granted Championship Status in 2012.

If you want to show your Savannah cat, therefore, the first thing you should do is familiarize yourself with TICA's published breed standard for the Savannah cat breed, and also with TICA's rules and regulations, and the requirements on how to register and join.

Savannah Cat Breed Standard

Savannahs were granted championship status by TICA in 2012, but with a few provisos. Any Savannah cat joining a cat show must be at least four months or age, is at least an F3 or further generation from the Serval, and must be of any of the permissible colors: Black Spotted Tabby (BST), Silver Spotted Tabby (SST), black, or smoke. In addition, the Savannah must be a C or SBT registered cat. This registration terminology means:

- "C" registered cats are the result of two "B" registered Savannahs. For "C" registered Savannahs, both the parents and the grandparents are Savannahs, but at least one grandparent is of a different breed.
- "B" registered Savannahs are the result of the cross between two "A" registered Savannahs. "B" registered Savannahs have both parents that are Savannahs, but at least one grandparent of a different breed.
- "A" registered Savannahs simply means that one parent is not a Savannah.
- When you cross two "C" registered Savannahs, what you have is an SBT, which stands for "Stud Book

Traditional." This means that there are three generations of Savannah to Savannah breeding in the cat's ancestry - the parents, the grandparents, and the great-grandparents.

"SBT"s are what are considered by TICA as "purebred" cats.

At present, Savannahs are being shown at the Advanced New Breed status. Only when enough SBT kittens are registered will Savannahs be moved to the Championship status, and "C" kittens will no longer be allowed to be shown. When this happens, only SBT Savannahs, or purebred Savannahs, will be shown.

Below is a summary of TICA's published Breed Standard for the Savannah Cat Breed.

General

The Savannah is tall, lean, and graceful, with striking dark spots and other bold markings on a background color of any shade of brown, silver, black, or black smoke. They closely resemble the African Serval, but are smaller in stature. They are affectionate, outgoing, with a long neck, long legs, tall ears, and a medium length tail.

Head, Chin, Nose, Muzzle and Neck

The face forms an equilateral triangle which is formed by the brow line, the sides following the jaw bone, and a rounded finish at the muzzle. Above this the forehead from the brow line and the tops of the ears form a rectangle. The head is small in proportion to the body.

The chin tapers to follow the triangle of the head; in profile, the nose protrudes slightly so the chin may appear recessed.

The nose is wide across the top, with low set nostrils. In profile, there is a slight downward turn at the end, giving a rounded appearance. The nose leather is slightly convex and wraps up over the nose.

The muzzle is tapered with no break. Whisker pads are not pronounced.

The neck is long and lean.

Ears

The ears are large and high on the head, wide and with a deep base. These are very upright and with rounded tops. Ideally, a vertical line can be drawn from the inner corner of the eye to the inner base of the ear. Ear furnishings may be present, pronounced ocelli (spots on the backs of the ears, or "eyes on the back of the head") are considered desirable.

Eyes

The eyes are medium in size, set underneath a slightly hooded brow. The top resembles a boomerang, set at an angle so that the corner slopes down the line of the nose. The bottom half of the eye has an almond shape. The eyes are low on the forehead, at least one eye's width apart. All eye colors are allowed and are independent of coat color.

Body, Legs, Feet and Tail

The torso is long, lean, well-muscled, with a full and deep rib cage, prominent shoulder blades, a slight tuck-up, and a rounded rump. The hip and thigh are full, long, and somewhat heavy.

The legs are longer than average, well-muscled, but not heavy or delicate. The back legs are longer than the front legs.

The feet are oval and medium in size.

The tail is medium to thick in width, medium in length, tapering slightly to a blunt end. Whippy tails are not desired.

Boning and Musculature

The boning is medium in density and strength.

The musculature is firm, well-developed, but smooth.

Coat, Coat Colors and Coat Patterns

The coat is short to medium in length, of good substance and with a slightly coarse feel. Coarser guard hairs cover a softer undercoat, and the spots are notably softer in texture than the guard hairs. The coat lies relatively flat against the body.

Acceptable coat colors are either solid, tabby, or silver/smoke, in colors ranging from black, brown (black), spotted tabby, black silver spotted tabby, and black smoke.

For black Savannahs, the nose leather must be solid black. Bold, solid markings are preferred in all tabbies, and in any variation, the lips are black, and tear duct lines are prominent. For spotted Savannahs, the nose leather can be pink to brick red, surrounded by a line, solid black, or black with a pink to brick center stripe. In either color variation, the paw pads are either deep charcoal or brownish black.

Only spotted patterns are accepted: either solid dark-brown or black spots, whether round, oval, or elongated. A series of parallel stripes run from the back of the head to just over the shoulder blades, fanning out slightly over the back. The spotting pattern follows the line of the stripes, with smaller spots on the legs and feet, as well as on the face.

For black Savannahs, ghost spotting may occur. For smoke Savannahs, a visible spotting pattern is preferred.

Temperament

The Savannah is confident, alert, curious, and friendly.

Penalties

The following are penalized: rosettes; spots in colors other than dark brown to black; distinct locket on the neck, chest, abdomen or any other area; vertically aligned spots or mackerel tabby type stripes; cobby body; and smallears

Disqualifications

Savannahs with extra toes are disqualified.

Any sign of challenge in temperament shall disqualify.

Registering Your Savannah with TICA

Because of the recent development of this hybrid breed, documentation and registration of Savannahs have been fairly easy and straightforward. Registered Savannah breeders are expected to register their cats or their kitten litters with TICA. This means that when you purchased your Savannah, either your cat must have already been registered, or you will receive a "blue slip" together with your kitten upon purchase. This blue slip is the breeder's litter registration form, which you can use to register your Savannah with TICA. If already registered, the breeder will sign over the registration papers to you, which you will also need to send off to TICA. In both instances, you will need to pay a small fee. Take note that if they come in the "non-standard" colors or coat patterns, you can still register them, though you may not be able to show them.

Preparing Your Savannah Cat for Show

The preparation of your Savannah for show must have already started long before the date of the show itself, ideally as kittens. First of all, any Savannah owner desiring to show their cat in a TICA show must make sure that their cat falls squarely within the classifications of acceptable Savannahs: either an F3 or later generation, a "C" or "SBT" registered cat, and possesses the acceptable coat colors and patterns of TICA. It might happen, therefore, that either you wished to show Savannah cats even when you purchased your kitten, and therefore looked for kittens that fell squarely under TICA's category of acceptable Savannahs for show, or you had no notion of showing when you purchased your kitten, but have been gratified later on to learn that your Savannah is acceptable for show on all points. Either way, preparing your Savannah for show must have started long before the show itself.

The preparation process itself is not different from preparing many other breeds of cats:

- A continuous socialization process ideally begun as kittens, so that your cat is not spooked, threatened, shy or timid around humans. Your Savannah will be handled by the judges during the show, so it is recommended that you get them used to being handled by several different people - in the same way that judges also handle show cats. A visit to a cat show will be very instructive.

- Steady nurturing and care in terms of health, diet, nutrition, and grooming. How healthy and how well-groomed your cat is during the show itself is the result of a lifetime of work: from careful attention to their diet and nutrition, regular veterinary and health checks, and regular and careful grooming. Grooming involves trimming nails, cleaning ears, regular brushing, brushing their teeth, and even bathing. Most show cats are, in fact, bathed prior to the date of the show itself (either a day or several days before the show), and you can only do this effectively if bathing is a habit that has been built over the cat's lifetime.

- Near the date of the show, you must already have learned the Breed Show standard by heart. This is because cat shows are not precisely a competition between cats to show which cat or cat breed is best. Cat shows aim to showcase cats that are the best or strong examples of their breed standards. And different breeds have different standards. How strong an example of the Breed Standard is your Savannah?

The next thing for you to do is gather relevant information: the schedules, dates and venues of the nearest TICA cat show, and the rules and regulations of TICA governing cat shows. Researching these should be fairly easy as there are a lot of informative guides on TICA's website. Some of TICA's show rules include:

- declawed cats shall not be penalized
- each entry should have its claws clipped prior to benching
- obviously pregnant cats or kittens are ineligible
- each cat has a single benching cage. Double cages and grooming spaces are available at additional cost

You might also want to pay a visit to one or more of these shows beforehand, just to see how things are conducted. Take note that Savannahs cannot be shown in the Household Pet (HHP) category, as New Trait or New Breeds are not allowed in HHPs.

When you're ready, here is a general procedure on how to join your first cat show:

- Check the nearest TICA show, the date, venue and requirements. Obtain an entry form, fill it in, and submit it together with the requisite fees.

- You will be receiving a confirmation. Check this carefully, and report any errors immediately prior to the event.
- Upon arrival at the show, your cat may be checked by a vet to confirm that it is not suffering from any illness, and has no signs of parasites such as mites, fleas, or fungal infections.
- You will be asked to show the confirmation papers, as well as a current vaccination certificate, so be sure to prepare these beforehand.

It is recommended that you arrive early as check-in lines can sometimes be quite long. Once you have finished checking in, you should proceed to the designated area where your cat is benched. You should begin setting up your cage curtains, the litter pan, and water dishes. Cage curtains are considered important as these gives your cat privacy. These may be simple or elaborate depending on your taste, as long as it fits the back, sides and top of the cage. Once you have finished setting up, relax, and enjoy the show.

You will probably not be able to leave the show while it is still ongoing, so here is a general checklist of things you should prepare beforehand to bring with you:

- cage curtains and clips
- litter and litter box

- food and water bowls
- nail clippers
- grooming equipment
- confirmation receipt
- vaccination records
- registration papers

Chapter Ten: Keeping Your Savannah Cat Healthy

The general consensus is that Savannah cats are one of the healthiest and hardiest breed of felines. To date, they have no known breed-specific problems. But this is not a guarantee of absolute good health. They can still be prone to many of the deady diseases afflicting the feline population, and for which they should receive the appropriate vaccinations, if available.

And because the development of the Savannah cats as a hybrid breed is fairly recent - it will take more time before experts can agree on what are or are not breed-specific health conditions among Savannahs. That said, there are a few health conditions that have appeared in some Savannahs, and which Savannah owners should be on the alert for.

Potential Health Problems Affecting Savannah Cats

Like most other cats, Savannahs should be screened before breeding to rule out potential incidences of hereditary and non-hereditary health conditions. There have been certain incidences of Savannah cats being diagnosed with the following conditions, though their prevalence in the breed as a whole has not yet been fully determined.

Some of the potential health conditions that may affect Savannah cats include:

- Hypertrophic Cardiomyopathy (HCM)
- Pyruvate Kinase (PK) Deficiency
- Taurine Deficiency

Hypertrophic Cardiomyopathy (HCM)

Hypertrophic Cardiomyopathy (HCM) is the most common heart disease seen in cats. This is a genetic condition, and is a concern among many purebreed cats. Cases of HCM have been found in some Savannahs, and it is recommended that breeders screen their breeder cats annually for HCM.

HCM is a condition which causes a thickening of the left ventricle of the heart. The left ventricle is responsible for receiving oxygenated blood from the lungs, pumping it to the aortic valve before it is distributed to the rest of the body. Because of this already demanding workload, the left ventricle is normally thicker than the right. But in cases of HCM, the left ventricle is abnormally enlarged or thickened, restricting bloodflow, thus causing the heart to work harder. There is usually an increased heart rate as a reflex as the body seeks to maintain blood pressure and cardiac output.

In some cats, there are no distinctive clinical signs of HCM, and the difficulty is that because it occurs more commonly among cats 5-7 years of age, it can only manifest itself after a cat has been bred. And since HCM can also manifest even after testing, annual screening important.

Some of the signs and symptoms to watch out for include:

- labored or rapid breathing

- lethargy
- open-mouthed breathing
- loss of appetite
- abnormal heart sounds or heart murmurs
- inability to tolerate exercise or exertion
- hind limb paralysis or signs of acute pain in the hind limbs
- sudden collapse

The variation in symptoms is caused by the varying effect of the thickening in the heart. Accumulation of fluid in or near the lungs can cause breathing or respiratory difficulties. Thromboembolism is caused by the development of a clot in the heart that when ejected into the system, can lodge in the periphery like the legs. This is what can cause pain or paralysis in the hind legs. And finally, the abnormal blood flow causes distinctive heart murmurs or abnormal heart rhythm.

Diagnosis is done through an echocardiograph or ultrasound imaging, which allows for a visual examination of the heart for signs of enlargement or thickening of the walls. This is currently the best method available for detecting HCM. Other possible diagnostic tools available is an electrocardiogram (EKG) and a Radiography (X-rays). A diagnosis of HCM can be made after ruling out hypertension and hyperthyroidism, which conditions can cause the same or similar symptoms.

There are medications available for HCM, depending on the severity and the symptoms.

- Beta-blockers for slowing down the heart rate
- Calcium-channel blockers for reducing the heart rate and contractions.
- ACE-inhibitors for congestive heart failure
- Aspirin and Warfarin to reduce the risk of blood clots
- Diuretics to remove excess fluid from the body
- Nitroglycerine ointment to dilate the vein and arteries

In severe cases, your cat may need to be hospitalized, kept in a stress-free environment and undergo oxygen therapy for difficulties in breathing.

Other things that you can do at home for your cat is to keep the environment safe and stress-free for your Savannah, restrict their sodium intake, and make sure that they avoid getting cold or chilled. Keep them in a reasonably warm room at all times. Make sure that they are brought to the vet at least every 6 months so that his condition can be monitored and any medication he is taking can be adjusted accordingly.

The prognosis of Savannahs diagnosed with HCM varies, as many of those with HCM may never develop any of the outward or clinical symptoms. On the other hand, congestive heart failure, thromboembolism, and hypothermia can signal poor prognosis, and may significantly decrease a cat's life span.

Pyruvate Kinase (PK) Deficiency or PKD

PK Deficiency should not be confused with PKD, or Polcystic Kidney Disease, which is different. PK Deficiency has been shown to be occur with significant frequency among several cat breeds, including the Savannahs. Other affected breeds include Abyssinian, Bengal, Domestic Shorthair and Longhair, Egyptian Mau, La Perm, Maine Coon, Norwegian Forest, Siberian, Singapura, and Somali cats. And because this is an inherited condition, offspring or crosses between and among these breeds are also at risk.

PK Deficiency is essentially an inherited condition in which the enzyme Pyruvate Kinase (PK) is missing or lacking. This enzyme is important for red blood cell energy metabolism, and its lack can lead to the instability and loss of red blood cells. Essentially, PK Deficiency is an inherited form of hemolytic anemia.

The onset of this condition is variable, and can manifest at any age. The symptoms are also variable, but can include severe lethargy, weakness, jaundice, weight loss, and abdominal enlargement. The severity of this condition can also vary, appearing as a mild and intermittent condition in some, but rapid and life-threatening in others.

There is a DNA test available to screen for this condition, and any prospective Savannah breeding cat must be screened for PK Deficiency. Depending on whether one or both parents are affected or are carriers, the offspring can also be carriers or be affected. This test is generally done by a simple mouth swab and the sample sent for laboratory analysis. In the results, your cat can either be clean, a carrier, or positive for PK Deficiency.

If positive, all is not necessarily lost. Some PK Deficiency positive cats can still live through its normal life span, showing only occasional signs of lethargy and anemia. It is a good idea to bring your cat to the vet so that you can map out potential medical treatment and and a rehabilitation plan, including lifestyle (diet and exercise) choices to address the symptoms. Needless to say, breeding from PK Deficiency-positive Savannahs is not recommended. In fact it is probably a good idea to inform the breeder from whom you have purchased your Savannah about the DNA results so that breeding from your cat's parents can also be discontinued - depending on whether one or both were carriers or affected.

Carrier cats are not likely to display any of the clinical signs of PK Deficiency, but it is a good idea to have them tested anyway. If they are confirmed carriers, breeding from them is also not advised - especially if they are paired with another carrier or another affected parent cat. There is still a chance that the condition might be carried on down the line. Being carrier, they can still live a long, happy, and healthy life - though of course they should no longer be included in breeding programs.

Taurine Deficiency

Savannah cats may be prone to Taurine Deficiency. This seems to be a nutritional inadequacy, and may be addressed quite effectively through diet and supplements, especially with kittens that are still in their developmental stages. Early on, particular attention should be paid to a Savannah cat's diet to guard against Taurine Deficiency.

Taurine is an amino acid that can be found in meats and fish, particularly in hearts and livers. High concentrations of Taurine can be found in meat, poultry, fish, and premium cat foods. They could not be found in vegetables, so feeding your Savannah a meat-based diet, or a meat-based cat food, is essential. It is theorized that the diet of cats in the wild - particularly the Savannah's ancestor, the Serval - is comprised, in a large part, by rodents. Servals were able to get all the Taurine that they needed from these rodents - whose brains were rich with this amino acid. While most cats require significant levels of Taurine in their diet, this may be a particular need for Savannahs due to the close proximity of their Serval heritage. At least, most breeders seem to agree that the Savannah's need for Taurine is greater than most other cats.

Taurine should be provided significantly in your Savannah's diet because cats, unlike other animals, derive their Taurine mostly from their diet. Cats cannot make enough Taurine internally for their needs, and if domesticated cats do not get enough Taurine from the food we feed them, Taurine Deficiency is almost always a certainty. In the 1970s, it was proven that many of the commercial cat foods at the time lacked sufficient Taurine, after many of the symptoms of Taurine Deficiency began appearing among domestic cats. Most major cat foods revised their formula to meet this need, but the difficulty is that some breeds seem to require more Taurine than others, and not all Taurine provides the same nutritional value. Some forms may be needed to be provided in larger volume for proper utilization and absorption by felines.

Taurine is an important nutritional need for cats. Among its uses are:

- it prevents dilated cardiomyopathy, or the failure of the heart muscle, or the inability of the heart muscle to meet the body's circulatory needs, thus swelling in the process

- promotes intestinal absorption of lipids (fats) as cholesterol
- prevents Feline Central Retinal Degeneration (FCRD), which is a progressive retinal disease among cats
- assists in reproductive processes, prevending incidence of still births, fewer than normal kittens, or fewer surviving kittens.

Some of the symptoms of Taurine Deficiency include:

- stunted growth
- the development of cardiomyopathy
- bones that do not develop properly
- loss of hair
- loss of teeth or tooth decay
- Taurine Deficiency in queens might produce kittens that are deformed or who die soon after birth; she may also produce a smaller litter than average, smaller-size kittens than average, or she might even inadvertently abort her fetuses
- Taurine Deficiency might also cause eye problems and irreversible blindness (Central Retinal Degeneration or CRD)

You can provide sufficient levels of Taurine to your cat through meats or meat-based diets or meat-based cat food, or additionally through supplements. Consult with your veterinarian to determine recommended amounts of Taurine for your Savannah kitten or cat, as dietary prescriptions and nutritional supplements should never be attempted without proper consultation and advice from your Vet.

Smaller Livers and Ketamine

Some veterinarians have noted that some Savannahs have inherited from Servals the tendency to have smaller livers relative to their body sizes. The precise medical effects of this has not yet been fully determined.

Some are of the opinion that greater care should be taken in the administration of medication such as the anesthetic Ketamine, which needs to be metabolized by the liver. Ketamine is often used in surgical procedures, and if your Vet is not familiar with the particular needs of Savannahs, breeders advise that you request that Isoflourine gas be used instead, or an injectable anesthetic protocol specific to exotic or hybrid bred felines. Using Ketamine, some breeders claim, may have potential ill effects that may sometimes even be lethal.

By contrast, many veterinarians are of the opinion that there is no particular difference between hybrid cats and other domestic cats that warrant different medical treatments, such as specific requirements in the use of anesthetic agents like Ketamine. Ketamine as an anesthetic cannot be used alone, and so perhaps the current opinion among many breeders of the dangers posed by Ketamine to Savannahs may have resulted from a misunderstanding of the drug and its administration. After all, they argue that Ketamine, used in servals and together with other specific elements, has already been proven safe.

The reader here is advised that while opinions on both sides are strong, there is no definitive proof either way. It is up to you to determine the particular needs of your Savannah, and if you feel that taking the safer route by avoiding Ketamine is preferred, you can certainly make this request of your vet. Perhaps it is best to seek out a veterinarian who specializes in, or has had some experience with hybrid breeds to begin with. Just make sure that any choice you make is an informed one, and is one that you are fully comfortable with.

Preventing Illness with Vaccinations

There has been much controversy regarding the do's and don't's of pet vaccinations in recent years, and many have held to strong but differing opinions. For a novice cat owner, it is difficult to sift through much of the recent debates, contrasting information, and strong sentiments from both pet owners and the veterinary community. How do you know which is which? Some pet owners who have seen for themselves the ill effects (or absence of ill effects) of vaccinations will have solid experience to back up their future judgments. But what about one who is bringing home a Savannah kitten for the first time?

In addition, there has been widespread opinion among Savannah breeders that Savannah cats should only be given killed vaccines, and never modified-live. There is also an addendum that Savannahs should not be vaccinated for FeLV (Feline Leukemia Virus) and FIP (Feline Infectious Peritonitus). These are based on reports of alleged bad side effects among Savannahs, and in the case of modified live vaccines, may even predispose the cat to contract the very disease they are being vaccinated against.

We say "alleged" because there have so far been no documented case or scientific finding to bolster these claims. And yet it might not cause any harm to take the safe and cautious route in such a volatile and confusing area of cat health care. Aside from the above precautions which Savannah breeders state are necessary, there does not seem to be any other differences between vaccination requirements of Savannah cats and other cat breeds.

If you are worried about the different advise, recommendations and opinions regarding vaccinations, the best thing to do is to sit down and have a conversation with your veterinarian. Most vaccination schedules - including the frequency of booster shots - will have to be adjusted anyway depending on your unique needs: your cat's state of health, age, lifestyle, medical history, state-required vaccines, and whether or not there are diseases currently prevalent and therefore threatening in your area or region. Don't hesitate to ask questions if there are things you don't understand, or if you have any doubts or worries.

As we proceed with this section on vaccinations, please take note that we are only providing general guidelines that are applicable to cats in general. The specific vaccines your cat will receive, and their frequency, will always vary depending on your unique circumstances. Don't forget that vaccines were developed to protect your cat's health, and have in fact saved many cats from what were once deadly and lethal diseases among the feline population.

Core Vaccines

Core vaccines are precisely what their name implies: necessary and obligatory vaccines for all cats, regardless of individual circumstances. They are designed to protect your cat from lethal diseases that are globally prevalent among cats.

The following are considered core vaccines:

- Rabies

- Feline viral Rhinotracheitis (FVR), also known as feline influenza
- Feline Calcivirus (FCV)
- Feline Panleukopenia Virus (FPV), also known as feline distemper

Non Core Vaccines

Non-core vaccines, on the other hand, are vaccines administered only depending upon need: whether or not the region, the lifestyle, or the local environment places the cat in greater risk of contracting any of the following:

- Chlamydophila felis
- Feline Leukemia Virus (FeLV)
- Feline Immunodeficiency Virus (FIV)
- Bordetella

Please take note that the following vaccines are **not** recommended in all circumstances. There is no evidence of their effectiveness, and an equally high possibility of adverse reactions.

- Feline Infectious Peritonitis (FIP)
- Giardia Lamblia

The table below shows a general schedule of vaccinations for kittens. Non-core vaccinations may be recommended based on the region where you lived and the risk of exposure. Core vaccinations will need to be boostered after a year, and then either one to three years afterwards, depending on the vaccine used.

Age	Core Vaccines
6-8 weeks	FVRCP Vaccine (Feline Viral Rhinotracheitis Calicivirus and Panleukopenia) Also recommended to start Heartworm Prevention
9-12 weeks	FVRCP Booster FELV Vaccine (Feline Leukemia Virus)
16 weeks	FVRCP Booster FELV Booster Rabies Vaccine

** Keep in mind that vaccine requirements may vary from one region to another. Only your vet will be able to tell you which vaccines are most important for the region where you live.

Savannah Cat Care Sheet

This final section is intended to provide you with a brief overview of many of the useful information contained in this book. It is a ready-reference resource that you can quickly skim through instead of reading the entire book, and will come in pretty handy if you simply want to refresh yourself regarding a few specific facts, or simply want a quick summary regarding the general contents of this book.

Or you may read below for a quick introduction to the Savannah cat breed before plunging into the rest of the book.

1.) Basic Savannah Cat Information

Pedigree: original cross between an African Serval and a Siamese domestic cat, also Bengals, Egyptian Maus, Oriental Shorthairs, Ocicats, and some average domestic shorthairs

Breed Size: varies depending on generation and sex; F1 hybrid males, and F1 and F2 generations, are considered the largest,

Weight: first generation Savannahs average at 8-20 lbs (6.3-11.3 kg); later generation Savannahs' average weight average at 7-15 lbs (3.17-6.8 kg.)

Body Type: long and leggy, tall and lanky

Coat Length: medium-length, spotted coat

Coat Texture: dense coat that can be either coarse or soft in texture

Coat Color: accepted colors are brown spotted tabby, silver spotted tabby, black, and smoke; other color patterns, though considered undesirable, include rosettes, marbles, white lockets, white toes

Eyes: medium sized eyes, set underneath slightly hooded brows; top of the eye resembles a boomerang, set at an angle so the corner of the eye slopes down the line of the nose, the bottom half has an almond shape

Ears: largest and high on the head, wide, with a deep base; upright and with rounded tips; they are considered the largest ears of all felines, in relationship to head size

Tail: short tail with black rings, and a solid black tip

Temperament: intelligent, energetic, exuberant, outgoing, demanding of human interaction

Strangers: friendly with strangers, either curious or playful

Children: tolerant and friendly with children, though exercise due caution and supervision, especially with infants and very small children

Other Pets: playful and gets along well with dogs and most other pets, but exercise due caution and supervision when it comes to smaller pets

Exercise Needs: needs daily exercise, sufficient vertical territory (cat trees), and daily interactive play with humans and/or other active pets

Health Conditions: generally healthy with no known genetic or breed-specific diseases or conditions

Lifespan: average 13-20 years

2.) Nutritional Needs

Nutritional Needs: water, protein, carbohydrate, fats, vitamins, minerals, amino acids

Calorie Needs: varies by age, weight, and activity level

Amount to Feed (kitten): feed freely but consult recommendations on the package

Amount to Feed (adult): consult recommendations on the package; calculated by weight

Feeding Frequency: four to five small meals daily

Important Ingredients: fresh animal protein (chicken, beef, lamb, turkey, eggs), animal fats, digestible carbohydrates (rice, oats, sweet potato)

Important Minerals: calcium, copper, iodine, manganese, magnesium, potassium, selenium, zinc, and phosphorus

Important Vitamins: Vitamin A, Vitamin C, Vitamin B, Vitamin D, Vitamin E, Vitamin K

Look For: AAFCO statement of nutritional adequacy; protein at top of ingredients list; no artificial flavors, dyes, preservatives

3.) Breeding Information

Sexual Maturity (female): average 5 to 6 months

Sexual Maturity (male): 5 to 8 months

Breeding Age (female): 12 months, ideally 18 to 24 months

Breeding Age (male): at least 18 months

Breeding Type: seasonally polyestrous, multiple cycles per year

Ovulation: induced ovulation, stimulated by breeding

Litter Size: about 3-4 kittens

Pregnancy: average 65 to 77 days

Kitten Birth Weight: variable depending on the generation, but can range from 110-125 grams (0.24 to 0.27 lbs.)

Characteristics at Birth: eyes and ears closed, little to no fur, completely dependent on mother

Eyes/Ears Open: 8 to 12 days

Teeth Grow In: around 3 to 4 weeks

Begin Weaning: around 4 to 6 weeks, kittens are fully weaned by 10 - 12 weeks

Socialization: between 8 and 13 weeks, ready to be separated by 14 weeks

Index

C

D

K

L

M

X

Y

Photo References

Page 1 Photo by skeeze via Pixabay.
<https://pixabay.com/en/savannah-cat-hybrid-serval-domestic-518126/>

Page 9 Photo by 3342 via Pixabay.
<https://pixabay.com/en/serval-small-cat-wildcat-predators-84082/>

Page 17 Photo by Leekimbud via Wikimedia Commons.
<https://commons.wikimedia.org/wiki/File:Scarlett%27s_Magic_Roaming.jpg>

Page 29 Photo by Savannah Clark via Wikimedia Commons.
<https://commons.wikimedia.org/wiki/File:Szavanna_macska_F5.jpg>

Page 41 Photo by skeeze via Pixabay.
<https://pixabay.com/en/savannah-cat-closeup-feline-hybrid-518134/>

Page 47 Photo by Nickolas Titkov from Moscow, Russian Federation via Wikimedia Commons.
<https://commons.wikimedia.org/wiki/File:SAV_%D0%90%D0%BB%D0%B8%D1%81%D0%B0_%D0%90%D0%BB%D1%8C%D1%8F%D1%80%D1%83%D1%81_(5624226102).jpg>

Page 57 Photo by Leekimbud via Wikimedia Commons. <https://commons.wikimedia.org/wiki/File:Kissing_Savanna hs.jpg>

Page 69 Photo by Galawebdesign via Wikimedia Commons. <https://commons.wikimedia.org/wiki/File:Savannah.jpg>

Page 77 Photo by Lifeatthesharpend via Wikimedia Commons. <https://commons.wikimedia.org/wiki/File:Savannah_Kitten s_F2b_1week_old.jpg>

Page 95 Photo by Leekimbud via Wikimedia Commons. <https://commons.wikimedia.org/wiki/File:Cat_USA.jpg>

Page 107 Photo by Camilla Hesby Johnsen via Wikimedia Commons. <https://commons.wikimedia.org/wiki/File:Savannah_kitten. jpg>

Page 123 Photo by DJC1970 via Wikimedia Commons. <https://commons.wikimedia.org/wiki/File:Iphone_039.JPG>

References

"A, B, C, SBT?" Select Exotics.
<http://savannahcatbreed.com/a-b-c-sbt/>

"About Savannah Cats." HP Savannahs.
<http://hpsavannahs.com/about-savannahs/>

"All About the Savannah Cat." Pet360.
<http://www.pet360.com/cat/breeds/all-about-savannah-
cats/7YuK-5sRHEWIUOVZdhDhjQ>

"Bengal Cat Health Corner." HWD Enterprises & Foothilll
Felines Bengals. <http://www.hdw-
inc.com/healthtaurine.htm>

"Bonding With Your New Kitten." WebMD.
<http://pets.webmd.com/cats/guide/bonding-with-your-
new-kitten>

"Bringing a Savannah Kitten Home." Select Exotics.
<http://savannahcatbreed.com/bringing-a-kitten-home/>

"Cardiomyopathy (heart disease) in cats." International Cat
Care. <http://icatcare.org/advice/cat-
health/cardiomyopathy-heart-disease-cats>

"Cat." Wikipedia. <https://en.wikipedia.org/wiki/Cat>

"Cat Food Tips to Make Your Wild Savannah Feel Right at Home." Donald Coggan. <http://www.the-savannah-cat.com/savannah-cat-food.html>

"Cat Grooming." WebMD. <http://pets.webmd.com/cats/guide/cat-grooming>

"Cat Grooming Tips." ASPCA. <http://www.aspca.org/pet-care/cat-care/cat-grooming-tips>

"Cat Nutrition Tips." APSCA. <http://www.aspca.org/pet-care/cat-care/cat-nutrition-tips>

"Cat Pregnancy Facts: How to Tell If Your Cat is Pregnant and More." PetMD. <http://www.petmd.com/cat/care/evr_ct_pregnant_cat>

"Cat Vaccination Schedule." petfinder. <https://www.petfinder.com/cats/cat-care/disaster-cat-vaccination-schedule/>

"Choosing a reputable and responsible breeder." CFHS. <http://cfhs.ca/athome/choosing_a_reputable_and_responsible_breeder_animals_for_sale_on_the_internet_or_in_the_newspaper/>

"Diet and Health Care." A1 Savannahs. <http://www.a1savannahs.com/cats/about-our-cats/about-savannah-cats/diet-and-health-care>

"Erythrocyte Pyruvate Kinase Deficiency (PK Deficiency) in Felines." UCDavis Veterinary Medicine.

<https://www.vgl.ucdavis.edu/services/pkdeficiency.php
>

"Everything About Newborn Kittens." Savannah Premium.
   <http://savannahpremium.com/USA/art1.html>

"FAQ." TICA's Savannah Breed Section.
   <http://www.savannahbreedsection.org/faq.php>

"Feline Vaccination." Wikipedia.
   <https://en.wikipedia.org/wiki/Feline_vaccination>

"Find a Breeder." TICA. <http://www.tica.org/find-a-
   breeder>

"Finding and Choosing a Purebred Cat Breeder." J. Anne
   Helgren.
   <http://www.petplace.com/article/cats/selecting-a-
   cat/adopting-or-buying-a-cat/finding-and-choosing-a-
   purebred-cat-breeder>

"Frequently Asked Questions." C and C Savannahs.
   <http://www.candcsavannahs.com/candcfaqs.htm>

"Frequently Asked Questions: Savannahs." Wild Trax
   Exotics.
   <http://www.wildaboutbengals.com/SVFAQ.htm>

"Good Health Makes for a Happy Savannah Cat and Owner
   Too!" Donald Coggan. <http://www.the-savannah-
   cat.com/savannah-cat-health.html>

"Heart Disease (Hypertrophic Cardiomyopathy) in Cats." PetMD. <http://www.petmd.com/cat/conditions/cardiovascular/c_ct_cardiomyopathy_hypertrophic#>

"Help! He's Not Using the Litterbox." Petfinder. <https://www.petfinder.com/cats/cat-behavior-and-training/cat-litterbox-training/>

"How Long Are Cats Pregnant - Symptoms of a Pregnant Cat!" Savannah Cat Breeders. <http://savannahcatbreeders-adela.blogspot.com/2011/09/how-long-are-cats-pregnant-symptoms-of.html>

"How Much Does a Savannah Cat Cost?" Lifestyle9. <https://lifestyle9.org/how-much-does-a-savannah-cat-cost/>

"How to Choose the Best Cat Food." PetMD. <http://www.petmd.com/cat/slideshows/nutrition-center/choosing-best-cat-food>

"How to Choose the Best Cat Food for Your Cat." Drs. Foster & Smith Educational Staff. <http://www.drsfostersmith.com/pic/article.cfm?aid=2695>

"How to Read Cat Food Labels." Kelli Miller. <http://pets.webmd.com/cats/guide/how-to-read-cat-food-labels>

"How to Recognize Taurine Deficiencies in Kittens."
Pets4Homes. <http://www.pets4homes.co.uk/pet-
advice/how-to-recognise-taurine-deficiencies-in-
kittens.html>

"How to Show." TICA. <http://www.tica-
uk.org.uk/html/how_to_show.html>

"Hypertrophic Cardiomyopathy (HCM)." College of
Veterinary Medicine at Washington State University.
<https://www.vetmed.wsu.edu/outreach/Pet-Health-
Topics/categories/diseases/hypertrophic-
cardiomyopathy-in-cats>

"Hypertrophic Cardiomyopathy (HCM). "Cornell State
University.
<http://vet.cornell.edu/hospital/Services/Companion/Car
diology/conditions/HCM.cfm>

"Hypertrophic Cardiomyopathy (HCM)." Stylisticat.
<http://www.stylisticat.com/hypertrophic-
cardiomyopathy-hcm.html>

"Kitten Socialization and Development." Petfinder.
<https://www.petfinder.com/animal-shelters-and-
rescues/fostering-cats/kitten-socialization/>

"Legal Restrictions for Savannah Cats Must Be Addressed
Before You Buy." Donald Coggan. <http://www.the-
savannah-cat.com/legal-restrictions-for-savannah-
cats.html>

"Litter Box 101: Preventing and solving litter box problems." Animal Humane Society. <https://www.animalhumanesociety.org/training/litter-box-101-preventing-and-solving-litter-box-problems>

"Mission Statement and Goals." TICA. <http://www.savannahbreedsection.org/mission.php>

"Online Breeder Listing." TICA. <http://forms.logiforms.com/formdata/user_forms/17237_4346552/78856//page1.html?isV2EmbedCode=true&cachebust=4825>

"Owning and Keeping Wild Cat Hybrids in the USA." Sarah Hartwell. <http://messybeast.com/small-hybrids/ownership-hybrids-usa.htm>

"Pyruvate Kinase Deficiency." Langford Veterinary Services. <http://www.langfordvets.co.uk/diagnostic-laboratories/diagnostic-laboratories/general-info-breeders/list-genetic-tests/pyruvate>

"Pyruvate Kinase Deficiency (PK Def)." Stylisticat. <http://www.stylisticat.com/pyruvate-kinase-deficiency-in-cats---pk-def.html>

"Savannah." cattime.com. <http://cattime.com/cat-breeds/savannah-cats>

"Savannah." TICA. <http://tica.org/cat-breeds/item/260-savannah-introduction>

"Savannah." vetstreet.
<http://www.vetstreet.com/cats/savannah#history>

"Savannah (SV)." TICA.
<http://tica.org/pdf/publications/standards/sv.pdf>

"Savannah Breed History." Cynthia A. King.
<http://www.kasbahsavannahcats.com/savannah-breed-history/>

"Savannah Breed History." TICA's Savannah Breed Section.
<http://www.savannahbreedsection.org/history.php>

"Savannahs." ChSavannahs.
<http://chsavannahs.com/en/savannahs/>

"Savannah Cat." Cat Breeds Information.
<http://catbreedsinformation.com/savannah-cat/>

"Savannah Cat." PetMD.
<http://www.petmd.com/cat/breeds/c_ct_savannah>

"Savannah Cat." Wikipedia.
<https://en.wikipedia.org/wiki/Savannah_cat>

"Savannah Cats." F1Hybrids Savannahs.
<http://www.f1hybridssavannahcats.com/learn/>

"Savannah Cat and Dog Vaccinations." Georgetown Veterinary Hospital.
<http://www.savannahanimalhospital.net/savannahcatanddogvaccinations.html>

"Savannah Cat Care." Wild Tafari.
   <http://wildtafari.com/Care.html>

"Savannah Cat Care & FAQ." Urban Safari.
   <http://www.urbansafaricattery.com/savannahcare.html>

"Savannah Cat FAQs." Afrikhan.
   <http://savannahconnection.com/savannah-cat-faqs/>

"Savannah Cat History." F1hybrids Savannahs.
   <http://www.f1hybridssavannahcats.com/breed/history>

"Savannah Cats 101." Before It's News.
   <http://beforeitsnews.com/animals-
   pets/2013/05/savannah-cats-101-2447680.html>

"Savannah Cats and Bengal Cats Make Bad Pets." BCR.
   <http://bigcatrescue.org/savannah-cats-and-bengal-cats-
   make-bad-pets/>

"Savannah FAQ." Allearz Savannahs.
   <http://www.allearzsavannahs.com/savannah-faq.html>

"Savannah Terminology." TICA.
   <http://www.savannahbreedsection.org/filialgenerations.
   php>

"Showing Your Cat." Brigitte Cowell.
   <http://www.kasbahsavannahcats.com/showing-your-
   cat/>

"Showing Your Cat in TICA." TICA.
   <http://www.tica.org/showing-cats>

"Socializing Your Kitten." CatTime. <http://cattime.com/cat-facts/kittens/82-kitten-socialization>

"Taurine Deficiency in Cats." PetMD. <http://www.petmd.com/cat/conditions/cardiovascular/c_ct_taurine_deficiency>

"The Decision to Breed." Veterinary & Aquatic Services Department, Drs. Foster & Smith. <http://www.peteducation.com/article.cfm?c=1+2139&aid=891>

"The Desirable and Expensive Savannah Cat." Pets4Homes. <http://www.pets4homes.co.uk/pet-advice/the-desirable-and-expensive-savannah-cat.html>

"The Savannah." Northwest Savannahs. <http://webup.com/nwsavannahs/breed.html>

"Tips for Socializing Your Kitten with People & Other Pets." Hill's Pet Nutrition. <http://www.hillspet.com/en/us/cat-care/new-pet-parent/socializing-kittens>

"Tips on Finding The Perfect Kitten." TICA. <http://www.tica.org/pdf/publications/brochures/kitten.pdf>

"Weaning Kittens: How and When." PetMD. <http://www.petmd.com/cat/centers/kitten/nutrition/evr_ct_weaning_kittens_what_to_feed_a_kitten>

"What Do You Know About Cat In Heat?" Must Love Cats. <http://www.mustlovecats.net/Cat-In-Heat.html>

"What is it like to have a Savannah (cat) as a pet?" Denise Terry. <https://www.quora.com/What-is-it-like-to-have-a-Savannah-cat-as-a-pet>

"When to Bring Your Savannah Kitten Home." Jennifer Miller. <http://www.savannahcatclub.com/docs/When-to-bring-a-savannah-home.pdf>

"Why Are Savannahs So Expensive." Snow Canyon Savannahs. <http://www.snowcanyonsavannahs.com/#!pricing-pay-pal-hybrid-laws/c1se>

Your Guide to Socializing a Kitten." Mikkel Becker. <http://www.vetstreet.com/our-pet-experts/your-guide-to-socializing-a-kitten>